Let Us Make Man

LET US MAKE MAN

★

Linleigh J. Roberts

THE BANNER OF TRUTH TRUST

THE BANNER OF TRUTH TRUST
3 Murrayfield Road, Edinburgh EH 12 6EL
P.O. Box 621, Carlisle, Pennsylvania 17013, U.S.A.

★

© *Linleigh J. Roberts 1988*
First Published 1988
ISBN 0 85151 525 8

★

★

Typeset in 10½/12pt Linotron Plantin
at The Spartan Press Limited,
Lymington, Hants
Printed and bound in Great Britain by
Hazell Watson & Viney Limited,
Member of the BPCC Group,
Aylesbury, Bucks

Contents

TO MY FAITHFUL MINISTERIAL
COLLEAGUES IN AUSTRALIA AND
NEW ZEALAND WHO LABOR FOR THE
FURTHERANCE OF THE GOSPEL.

Introduction

Knowing that Americans do not always follow traditional methods, my students at Evangelical College of Biblical Studies in Australia looked me over carefully when I entered the classroom for the first time. I had grown up in Australia and understood their apprehension; I could almost feel their questions and uncertainty. What would this 'Americanized' teacher do? What would he expect? They were utterly speechless when I told them we would begin with an exam. Being accustomed to a traditional British educational system, exams were reserved for the end of term, not the beginning! Since it was the senior class in theology, I was concerned to know what they had already learned. My questions were simple and straightforward; I asked such things as: 'What is sin?', 'Who is Jesus Christ?', 'What is justification?', and 'What is God?'. Sad to say, I was disappointed in their answers; generally, they were simplistic Sunday School clichés. I soon discovered, however, that those students were well informed in world religions, contemporary theology, and cults, but they did not understand the faith they professed to believe. A Pakistani minister visited the college that year. His comment to me concerning theological education in Australia summed up the situation. He said, 'Barth we know and Bultmann we know but who is Jesus and who is Paul?'

Because the theological understanding of my students was at best elementary, their efforts at proclaiming the gospel were both deficient and unfruitful. We cannot expect the world to abandon a deeply ingrained philosophy, no matter how deficient, for a disordered presentation of clichés. Realizing their need, I dispensed with my class schedule and began to deal with the basic doctrines of the Christian faith. After only two or three weeks of

I

discussion on 'What is God?' (some of them had been bold enough to change the question on the test to read 'Who' rather than 'What'), they began to witness with a new zeal and enthusiasm. It was thrilling to see them witness for Christ with confidence as they realized that the Christian faith is built upon sound facts and sufficient evidences.

Subsequently, my ministerial responsibilities have taken me into numerous Christian homes and churches in Australia, New Zealand and the United States. It has been my privilege to meet many fine Christian people and to preach in the pulpits of most denominations. I have thoroughly enjoyed the fellowship and, in many cases, the hospitality of their homes. Through this exposure to many of God's people, I have learned a great deal about Christian love and grace (I have often prayed that these virtues were as evident in my life). Sad to say, I have learned also that a simplistic understanding of the Christian faith is not confined to that class of students in Australia. Unfortunately, it is not confined to laymen either; there are many pastors who have never grasped the significance of many of the basic Christian doctrines.

At the outset, we need to realize that there is no substitute for knowledge. Christian virtues are important and we must give diligence to cultivate them in our lives, but it is futile to attempt to do so apart from a knowledge of the truth. It is impossible to grow the flowers of grace and love without the soil of truth. In other words, virtues do not exist very long out of their proper context or environment. In these days there are many who attempt to generate excitement in the heart which is unrelated to knowledge in the head; but this will never produce conviction in the mind, confidence in the heart, or stability in character. The lack of knowledge is cause for deep concern; one recalls the words of God through his prophet, 'My people are destroyed for lack of knowledge' (*Hos. 4:6*). Perhaps as never before, Christians today need to realize that 'we did not follow cleverly devised tales' or 'worldly fables fit only for old women' (*2 Pet. 1:16; 1 Tim. 4:7*). God has given us a book of truth, through which we are enlightened, restored, warned, and sanctified (see *Ps. 19:7–11* and *John 17:17*). It is through that book of truth that we know God; and 'the people who *know* their God will display strength and take action' (*Dan. 11:32*; my emphasis).

It is important to realize also that the Bible is not a random collection of ideas or facts; it is a wonderfully coherent body of truth. Naturally, some truths or doctrines are more important than others, but that does not mean some truths can be ignored. If God has revealed a truth, it is important; it is equally important to see how that truth fits into the total picture. We are dealing with the '*whole* counsel of God'.

Because of my deep concern for many of my fellow believers and because many of them have requested it, I have undertaken to write this book. I have tried to keep it simple and uncomplicated so that Christians at all levels of spiritual growth and maturity will profit. I have, however, written with the young or immature believer in mind. I have written for those many friends and acquaintances who do not have the benefit of sound biblical teaching in their local church. My purpose is to set forth the basic truths of salvation and to show how those truths relate to each other and to life in order that other members of the body of Christ might 'rejoice in the truth', be 'strong in the Lord', and 'take action' for him. I long that believers everywhere will have firm convictions in their minds, godly enthusiasm in their hearts, and bold confidence in their witness. To that end I pray God will use these pages.

PART I

Man – as God Made Him

1: *Man as God Made Him*

Several years ago, a missionary and I were scheduled to speak at a family Bible conference in the South Island of New Zealand. When we met and he learned I was Principal (President) of Evangelical College, he asked, 'What does your College teach about man?' As he came from Europe, the cradle of the Reformation, one might have expected him to ask about our views on the sovereignty of God. Or, being in New Zealand, where most churches have been influenced by the charismatic movement, he might have asked about our views of the Holy Spirit. Or, being aware of contemporary theological trends, he could have asked what our position was on the inerrancy of the Bible. Instead, he asked about our view of man. Why? He did so because he was a man of real perception. He understood that our concept of man affects our view of salvation, our methods of evangelism, and our hope for the future. Indeed, it affects everything.

The world today has a low view of man's origin. It affirms that human beings emerged from pre-historic barbarians through an evolutionary process. Though some, like Teilhard de Chardin, have tried to find meaning and purpose in these evolutionary origins and to explain how evolution has produced continual development and improvement, such explanations are hollow and unsatisfactory. It is not possible to find purpose or meaning in evolution because the entire theory depends upon *chance*. When everything is governed by chance, there is no possibility of order, purpose, or direction. The distorted view of man held by modern society demands that the Christian understand the biblical view clearly and be able to present it logically and forcefully.

The Bible presents a far more satisfactory view than the

7

evolutionary theory. When God created the heavens and the earth, he spoke the word and it was done (*Ps. 33:9; Heb. 11.3*). The creation of man, however, was a unique act. We are told that 'the Lord God formed man of dust from the ground' (man is, therefore, directly *identified* with creation), and that God 'breathed into his nostrils the breath of life; and man became a living being' (he is, therefore, *separate*, or set apart, from the rest of creation) (*Gen. 2:7*). We may say reverently: God was not playing or experimenting, nor was he deciding what to do as he proceeded. That is unthinkable! When the Bible declares that man is made *by* God, it implies purpose and plan. It not only states that man is made by God, however; it states that man is made *like* God (*Gen. 1:27*); such statements imply that man has special honor and dignity. Man has a meaningful origin; without that, it is impossible to find meaning for his present existence. In making man, God had a wonderful purpose. To discover that purpose, it is necessary to consider what it means to be made in God's image.

The Westminster Shorter Catechism brings biblical facts together when it states:

God created man male and female, after his own image, in knowledge, righteousness, and holiness, with dominion over the creatures.[1]

Because this definition is so basic and important, we need to consider it in detail.

I. MAN IS MADE IN THE IMAGE OF GOD
IN KNOWLEDGE

Solomon said, 'It is not good for a person to be without knowledge' (*Prov. 19:2*). When God created Adam, he did not make him with an intellectual vacuum, without knowledge. God did not make Adam with just the ability to think or the capacity for knowledge. God gave Adam a true understanding of the world in which he lived. Undoubtedly, Adam's knowledge was not exhaustive, but what he knew about God, about himself, and about the creation was accurate. We know this to be true from Paul's statement to the Colossians: 'put on the new self who is being renewed to a true

[1] The Shorter Catechism, Question 10.

8

knowledge according to the image of the One who created him' (*Col. 3:10*). If we are being '*renewed* to a true knowledge according to the image' of God, knowledge must have been an original gift of God.

Knowledge is complex, like a jigsaw puzzle. Several years ago, one of my Christmas presents was a 2,000-piece puzzle of Linderhof Palace in Germany. I opened the box, emptied the contents on the table and began sorting the pieces. Before long I became suspicious that the puzzle I was working on bore no resemblance to the picture on the box. That puzzle proved to be quite difficult because I had to construct it without any guide or reference point. Actually, it turned out to be a picture of a farmer with his horse and wagon! When working on a puzzle, I usually sort out the corner pieces, study the picture, and then proceed to construct the border. Once the border is there, I have a framework into which all the other pieces fit.

As we go through life, we constantly pick up pieces of information; ultimately, all these pieces must fit together into one comprehensive picture (we live in the *uni*verse, not a *multi*verse!). In order to put each piece of information or knowledge into its proper place, it is essential to have a reference point or guide. Of course, even when we have the total picture before us, it is not always easy to determine where a particular piece of information fits. Sad to say, there are many people who have the wrong picture or no picture at all and thus have no idea what they are constructing. The problem is that we need knowledge; we cannot live without it. We need not only the pieces but a reference point. In other words, we need content (pieces) and a context (framework). Adam, as God made him, had both.

The Bible informs us that when God made Adam, he gave him the responsibility to name all the animals in the garden. That is significant. To us, the naming of animals, and even our children, is an arbitrary personal choice. We choose names which appeal to us. In Old Testament days it was quite different; to name was to designate or classify. Often a name was a description of the nature or character; it was not uncommon for a name to be changed when there was a change of character. For example, Jacob (supplanter) was renamed Israel (prince with God) after his personal encounter with the Lord. For Adam to name the animals, therefore, necessitated accurate knowledge about each of the species. He knew the facts; he had the pieces.

Adam had not only an accumulation of assorted facts but also the right reference point or framework. He saw things in relationship to God. We are told that God walked with Adam in the garden; no doubt that was a time of fellowship and instruction. Though Adam possessed knowledge, he needed to learn. He needed to increase in knowledge. As God made him, however, Adam had the right facts and the right framework; he had the right content and the right context. God made Adam a *rational* being; he was made in the image of God in knowledge.

Knowledge is primary. The scripture says about man, 'as he thinks within himself, so he is' (*Prov. 23:7*). What we think (content) and how we think (context) determine what we are (character) and what we do (conduct). To be right, we must think right. Wrong thinking will never produce right living. Good character and righteous conduct are dependent upon true and accurate knowledge. Adam possessed accurate knowledge; that makes his fall exceedingly tragic. He sinned against the knowledge he possessed. Since the fall, God has given his word to men; it provides us with the right framework into which all the pieces of knowledge fit. The Bible shows us how the facts are to be integrated into one comprehensive picture; it shows us how all things relate to God, the Creator. We will discuss this further at the appropriate point. Here, I want to establish the fact that God has made us *rational* beings; he has given us *minds* in order to think and know the truth.

II. MAN IS MADE IN THE IMAGE OF GOD IN
RIGHTEOUSNESS AND HOLINESS

Ephesians 4:24 speaks of 'the new self, which in the likeness of God has been created in righteousness and holiness'. If the new man is being made in righteousness and holiness after (or like) God, then these must have been original attributes of man as God made him. Righteousness is sometimes used to describe actions, but I use it here as a description of character.

Righteousness and holiness are not arbitrary qualities dependent upon subjective or relative opinions. The meaning of these qualities is based upon and derived from the character of God. God is a moral God: he is 'infinite, eternal, and unchangeable, in his . . . holiness, justice, goodness, and truth'.[1] Because he is infinite, eternal, and unchangeable in these moral attributes, he is the moral standard by which we must measure ourselves. God is morally perfect; he demands that we be morally perfect also.

When God made Adam, he did not make him morally neutral. Many people view their children in this way; they consider them to be morally neutral when they are born and to remain that way until they reach an age of moral accountability. That is not true. Our children are morally accountable, no matter what their age. When God made Adam, he made him holy, just, good, and true. Adam not only had the characteristics of God (that is, the capacity to be righteous and holy); he had the character of God (that is, he possessed the qualities of godliness). Because he was made morally perfect, his innermost desires and motivation were holy and right. His moral condition was not a separate entity all by itself. It was related directly to his knowledge. He *knew* what was good and right and he *desired* what was good and right. 'As he thinks within himself, so he is' (*Prov. 23:7*). Adam was not only a rational being; he was made a *moral* being also. And, in this area of morals, we are dealing with the *desires* or *emotions*.

III. MAN IS MADE IN THE IMAGE OF GOD
TO HAVE DOMINION

God said to Adam, 'Be fruitful and multiply, and fill the earth, and subdue it; and rule [have dominion] over . . . every living thing that moves on the earth' (*Gen. 1:28*). When God made man, he did so for a definite purpose. What was that purpose?

Man's chief end [purpose] is to glorify God and to enjoy him for ever.[2]

What is meant by 'glorify'? In a *general* sense, it means to recognize God's sovereignty over all things. It means to worship him, that is, to recognize his worth. And, having recognized his

[1] *Ibid.*, Question 4.
[2] *Ibid.*, Question 1.

worth, to love him fervently and to serve him faithfully. It means to accept his instructions without hesitation, question or complaint. In a *particular* sense, to glorify God means to utilize fully the gifts, talents, and resources he has given in such a way that his name is hallowed, his kingdom extended, and his will done on earth. In other words, God gives each individual different gifts and resources, and he is glorified when a person uses what God has bestowed in the fulfillment of his wonderful purpose.

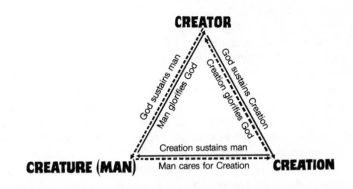

In order to fulfill God's purpose, we must know and desire that purpose. As Adam tended the garden (*Gen. 2:15*) according to God's command, he was fulfilling the purpose for which he had been made. God purposely planned for the natural creation to sustain man and to give him enjoyment. On the other hand, God made man to care for the creation in a way that would honor God. From the general tenor of scripture, I believe that when God made Adam, he made him to work systematically, consistently, and industriously towards specific objectives. He knew the dignity of work and the satisfaction of accomplishment. To do the will of God is always purposeful, satisfying, and fulfilling because that is the reason we were made. God did not make square pegs for round holes.

When God made man, he created him in his own image as a being with *purpose*. Here, it is not the mind or the emotions which are primarily involved; it is the *will*.

This underlines the fact that we are considering the *whole* man:

Man – as he thinks – involves the mind.
Man – as he is (character) – involves the desires.
Man – as he acts – involves the will.

Man is made in the image of God; he is, therefore, a wonderful being. We need to understand, however, that his value or worth does not lie in what he is. He is made of the dust of the earth; he has no intrinsic value. His worth lies in the fact that he is made in his Maker's image. I have a picture of my wife in my study; actually, that picture is only a piece of paper of very little value. What makes it valuable is that it bears the image of the one I love. This needs to be understood clearly in our day, when there is so much talk about self-esteem and self-love. We need to realize how valuable we are; many of our problems are due to poor self-image – so we are told. This is not a biblical perspective. Man is valuable only because he bears the image of his Maker. In Genesis chapter 9, murder is a capital crime because an attack upon man is an affront to the image of God (*Gen. 9:6*). Man is wonderful only because he is made *by* God, *like* God, and *for* God. Sin, however, has entered the picture and to that we must now turn our attention.

Man, made in God's image, has	Scripture	He is a	Faculty	Man, as he
Knowledge	Col. 3:10	*Rational being*	Mind	Thinks
Righteousness & Holiness	Eph.4:24	*Moral being*	Desires	Is (Character)
Dominion	Gen. 1:28	Being with *purpose*	Will	Acts (Conduct)

PART II

Man – as Sin Made Him

2: *What Adam Did*

My mother died an agonizing death with cancer at the age of forty-eight. So far as I know, there was no point during her illness at which her faith wavered; she faced eternity with confidence, and she rejoiced in the expectation of seeing her Lord face to face. Her dying words were those of the hymn-writer: 'Sweet will of God, still fold me closer/Till I am wholly lost in Thee.'[1] Though she and my father assured the doctors that she knew God personally and was therefore not afraid to die, the doctors refused to tell either of them the truth about her condition. It is, of course, an accepted procedure in the medical profession to conceal the truth about a patient's condition if it is feared the emotional response will aggravate the problem. There are times when the truth really hurts, and we cannot cope with it. One thing worse than having cancer in the body is having cancer in the soul. The truth about soul cancer is painful to contemplate; indeed, if you want to see people get emotionally upset, just begin to talk to them about sin. Many psychologists and psychiatrists have devised ways to avoid the problem or at least to divert attention away from it; those who take a biblical approach and meet the problem head on are not popular, even in Christian circles. However, unlike a physical problem, we cannot commit our spiritual problems into the hands of a professional and trust him to do what he thinks is right. The only way to spiritual health is to face the problem of sin. It will not go away by rationalizing it, projecting it, or compensating for it. Forgiveness and cleansing from sin come only when we acknowledge our true condition before God. David said, 'I acknowledged my sin to Thee, and my iniquity I did not hide; I

[1] *Hymns of the Christian Life* (Harrisburg, Pa., Christian Publications, 1978), Hymn 261.

said, "I will confess my transgressions to the Lord"; and Thou didst forgive the guilt of my sin' (*Ps. 32:5*). Forgiveness is contingent upon confession.

Although sin is a subject we would much rather avoid, we cannot do so; we must face it and face it honestly. We must understand how sin has affected us. A weak view of sin inevitably leads to a weak view of salvation. In other words, if we do not realize how serious the problem is, we will fail to seek an adequate remedy. Apparently, it is not uncommon for a man having a heart attack to say, 'It is nothing much; just a bit of indigestion. I'll be alright in a minute.' Many defer or even refuse the help they need because they do not realize how serious their condition really is. Sin is much more serious than most of us realize; if we knew, we would waste no time seeking the help of the Great Physician.

To understand the nature and problem of sin, we must, first of all, understand what Adam did. If Adam had been a barbaric cave-man with animal instincts, as modern evolutionists portray him, his sin would have been neither significant nor serious. We would attribute his sin to instincts that are now being refined and overcome. Men today have a low view of man's origin, and therefore, a superficial view of sin. As we have noted previously, man is wonderful; he is made in the image of God. Sin, therefore, is terrible and tragic. The point is this: if we are to grasp the magnitude of Adam's fall, we must understand who has fallen. We must see man as God made him if we are to understand man as sin has made him.

When I began ministering in the pastorate, I was asked to teach the teenagers the doctrines of our faith. Naturally, I began with the doctrine of sin and then proceeded to discuss the doctrines of election, the atoning work of Christ, God's grace, and finally, the doctrine of eternal security. Eternal security is, of course, the doctrine dealing with the question, 'Can a person be lost after he has been saved?'. The class went along smoothly until we came to that question. At that point, I was inundated with all kinds of questions. I soon realized, however, that the questions being asked did not begin in the doctrine of eternal security; they had their roots in the doctrine of sin. Because I had not dealt adequately with the doctrine of sin, my students had problems with all the doctrines of the Bible. I have since come to realize that the doctrine of sin is the Great Divide in theology. What we believe about sin will determine what we think about the Savior and what we believe about salvation.

We saw in the previous chapter that man is made in the image of God as a rational, moral and purposive being. We are dealing with the *whole* man: his mind, his emotions or desires, and his will. How has sin affected the *whole* man? If we fail to see how sin has touched all these areas, we will come down on one side of the Great Divide; if we see that it has affected the whole man, we will come down on the other side. If sin has only partially affected man, there is some possibility that man can have some part in his salvation. This is the major difference between Arminian and Reformed theology. It has tremendous consequences: either our salvation is in the hands of God or it is in the hands of man himself.

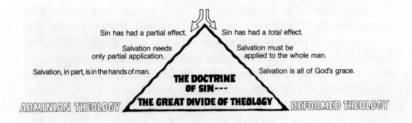

The Shorter Catechism asks the question, 'Did our first parents *continue* in the estate wherein they were created?' (my emphasis). The answer is: 'Our first parents, being left to the freedom of their own will, fell from the estate wherein they were created, by sinning against God.'[1] Sometimes it is said that the name 'Adam' is a generic term for all mankind. A quick glance at Genesis 5:3–5 (not to mention a number of evidences in chapters 1–4) should dispel any doubts about Adam's identity and establish his historicity beyond question. In those verses we are told that Adam lived 130 years before begetting a son named Seth. After Seth was born, he begat other sons and daughters, lived another eight hundred years and finally died. That is rather hard to apply to mankind in general!

[1] The Shorter Catechism, Question 13.

storicity of Adam is significant and has far-reaching consequences. Adam stood at the head of the human race, and what he did affects us. He was our representative and, as the scripture informs us, 'through one man sin entered into the world' and 'through the one man's disobedience the many were made sinners' (*Rom. 5:12, 19*). If Adam had not been an individual, and if his act of disobedience had been mythical or allegorical rather than actual, we would have no adequate explanation for the existence of sin in the world today. While we might not like the fact that what Adam did affects us, it is, none the less, a fact clearly taught in scripture. What then, did Adam do?

I. WHAT ON EARTH WAS ADAM THINKING?

When Satan approached Adam and Eve, he did so at the 'tree of the *knowledge* of good and evil' (*Gen. 2:17*; my emphasis). His temptation was designed to appeal to the mind. It was an attractive and seemingly plausible proposition; it was reasonable. To follow Satan's advice appealed to Adam and Eve because it appeared as though they had the opportunity to become greater than they already were. They would not only be *like* God; they would be *as* God. Satan knew that to capture the human mind was to capture the whole man and everything which had been entrusted to his care.

Adam had the command of God. God's word then, as now, is the basis of life. 'Man does not live by bread alone, but man lives by everything that proceeds out of the mouth of the Lord' (*Deut. 8:3*). No man can ignore or disobey what God says and live. God's word to Adam was clear and explicit. What did Adam do with this word? He began to question it; then he rejected it. He 'exchanged the truth of God for a lie' (*Rom. 1:25*). Adam no longer considered God's word as the basis for his thinking; it was no longer his map and compass for life. The foundation – the framework, the context – for accurate thinking was gone. Since Adam considered himself to be as God, he now had to think independently without guidelines or a reference point other than himself.

Having exchanged and abandoned the word of God as the foundation and directive for life, Adam refused to retain God in his knowledge (see *Rom. 1:28 KJV*). He excluded God from his thinking. He now saw things in relationship to himself; he became the god of his own world. Paul in describing man says, they 'became futile in their speculations, and their foolish heart was darkened' (*Rom. 1:21*). He goes on to say, they 'worshiped and served the creature [himself] rather than the Creator' (*Rom. 1:25*). Being his own god, man worshiped himself and worked for himself. In describing men just prior to the flood of Noah's day, the scripture says, 'Every intent of the thoughts of his heart was only evil continually' (*Gen. 6:5*). Obviously, evil thoughts include matters which are morally corrupt, but they do not stop there. Evil thoughts include also those 'nice' thoughts we have of ourselves, but which exclude God.

So then, when 'our first parents . . . fell from the estate wherein they were created', they lost both the *context* and the *content* for accurate and true knowledge. The fall brought about a radical intellectual change.

II. WHAT ON EARTH HAPPENED TO ADAM?

In recent years, my home country changed from the use of imperial measurements to the use of the metric system. For some of us, it was quite an adjustment and, at times, very frustrating. I entered a store one day to see a cashier holding up a pair of men's trousers and asking the girl next to her, 'How big is 865?' At times the change-over was quite expensive. Imagine working on construction and discovering to your dismay that some of the bricks or lumber are standard and others are metric. Think of the problem of replacing a bathroom fixture and discovering that you have to replumb your entire house because fittings are no longer available. Consider the problem of having your speedometer graduated in miles and the road signs in kilometers! Standards are very important to us. Daily we find it necessary to appeal to such measuring devices as calendars, watches, rulers and tape measures, money, scales, thermometers, and speedometers. Measurements are very much a part of our daily lives.

Most of the measuring devices we use are not the kind of precision instruments which engineers building a spacecraft must use, but we understand that there is a bureau of weights and measurements where the absolute standard is kept. For any man to be judged as righteous or unrighteous, holy or unholy, there must be a standard by which he is measured. It is not uncommon to hear people say, 'I'm every bit as good as he is.' What they are doing, of course, is using themselves as the standard for goodness. To say the least, that is a very subjective and unreliable standard. We need an absolute standard which never changes. We need an objective moral standard. The only place where we can find an absolute for morals is, of course, in the character of God. He is morally perfect and he never changes. As *moral* beings, made in his image, we must measure ourselves alongside him.

When Adam sinned and 'fell from the estate wherein he was created' he set himself up as god. He determined to know good and evil without reference to the character of God. Ever since, men have been floundering in the murky waters of subjective morals, relative judgments, and situation ethics. Having rejected the character of God as the absolute standard, and set himself up in place of God, Adam no longer desired to do what was right and holy. His desires were, as the apostle described them, 'of the flesh and of the mind' (*Eph. 2:3*). He became prejudiced against righteousness and holiness. He 'loved the darkness rather than the light; for [his] deeds were evil' (*John 3:19*).

The fall brought about a radical moral change. Objectively, the only adequate standard of measurement was rejected. Subjectively, the desires of the heart became corrupt.

III. WHAT IN THE WORLD DID ADAM DO?

In 1969, my wife and I were given a trip to Europe. While we were in Germany I bought a sophisticated toy for one of my boys; it was something like an 'erector set', only much more elaborate. It was one of those toys which makes a father thankful he has a son to give him an excuse to buy it. One Saturday afternoon, one of my students came to our house, and together we built the most fascinating machine that was ever engineered. Our invention was powered by a little motor, and it did all kinds of wonderful things; wheels turned, arms went up and down, and light flashed. It was a marvelous machine. The only problem was that it had no purpose whatsoever. For many people, life is like that; their lives are filled with all kinds of activities, but they are going nowhere and accomplishing nothing. For them, life has no purpose.

God did not make man to be that way, however. We were made in God's image to have dominion. Adam was made to glorify God by caring for the creation, but the fall had a profound effect upon the fulfillment of that purpose. Having exchanged the truth of God for a lie, Adam was no longer able to discern God's purpose for his life. And, having become unrighteous and unholy, he no longer had any desire to discern God's purpose even if he had been able to. In other words, he had neither the understanding nor the character to fulfill the purpose for which God had made him. Because Adam had rejected the rule of God in his own life, he was unfit to rule God's creation. How could he command the creation when he rejected the command of God, the Creator?

God had made Adam to rule the creation in such a way that God would be glorified. Having been committed to his care, the creation was to be used wisely and handled righteously. Adam was to be a good steward of all that God had entrusted to him. Instead, he chose to 'do his own thing' and he began to exploit the creation for his own ends. Someone has said, 'God made man to love people and use things; instead he loves things and uses people.' Instead of doing the will of God and fulfilling the purpose for which he had been made, Adam determined to do his own will. His will and the will of God came into direct opposition and conflict. To borrow a phrase from the New Testament, he 'set at nought dominion'; or, as the apostle Peter expressed it, he despised dominion (see *2 Pet. 2:10 ASV*).

So then, there are two elements involved here. Objectively, Adam rejected the command of God and therefore God's purpose for his life. Subjectively, he set his will in direct opposition to the will of God. What were the consequences? Or, as the Shorter Catechism asks, 'Into what estate did the fall bring mankind?' The answer is: 'The fall brought mankind into an estate of sin and misery.'[1] 'What is sin?' 'Sin is any want of conformity unto, or transgression of, the law of God'[2] (see also *1 John 3:14*). Adam had the command of God. He transgressed it and, in so doing, turned away from the purpose for his existence. Man is now involved in all

[1] *Ibid.*, Question 17.
[2] *Ibid.*, Question 14.

23

kinds of activities which are empty and without any real purpose. God, in his great mercy, has given us his word, his commandments, in which we can discover his will and purpose. While we persist in transgressions and live in disobedience, we can expect misery, both in this life and in the life to come.

Man as God made him	What Adam did	Objective (outward)	Subjective (inward)
Knowledge	He exchanged the truth of God for a lie	He rejected God's word as the foundation for life	His mind became set against God
Righteousness & Holiness	He followed the way which seems right	He rejected God's character as the standard for morals	His desires were 'of the flesh'
Dominion	He set at nought dominion	He rejected God's will as the purpose for life	His will was set in opposition to the will of God

3: *What Man Is Because Of What Adam Did*

Having seen what Adam did and how his sin affected him totally, we must now consider what impact his sin and rebellion have had upon us. Some people find it difficult to comprehend how one simple act done thousands of years ago can have any bearing on us at all. Adam's sin seems so remote. It is a fact of life, however, that the decisions we make and the direction we travel in life both have consequences for our children.

I do not know how authentic some of my family history is; it could have been whitewashed and embellished as it has been handed down the generations. However, the story is that my great-great-grandfather was in his late teens in England when he met a friend one evening who had a rabbit in his coat that he had just poached from the commons. Both of them were apprehended by the authorities, placed on a convict ship, and transported to Australia. A simple decision to walk down the street brought a radical change in our family history.

'Did all mankind fall in Adam's first transgression?' Notice carefully the answer:

The covenant being made with Adam, not only for himself, but for his posterity; all mankind, descending from him by ordinary generation, sinned in him, and fell with him, in his first transgression.[1]

Let me ask the question a little more pointedly: 'Did all mankind, *without exception*, fall in Adam's first transgression?' The answer is 'No'. There is an exception; our Lord Jesus Christ was a descendant of Adam, and he did not sin. He was truly man but without sin. The Catechism answer, however, takes that fact into

[1]The Shorter Catechism, Question 16.

25

account; it speaks of those who descend from Adam *by ordinary generation*. The Lord Jesus Christ descended from Adam by *extraordinary* generation; he was conceived by the Holy Spirit and born of the virgin Mary. His birth was unique because he was unique. Had he been born of ordinary generation, he would not be unique and therefore he could never have been our Savior. Of course, sin is not a biological thing inherent in the genes; it is a moral issue. As we shall see later, he had to be one of us but unaffected by Adam's transgression.

The scriptures are clear: 'Just as through one man sin entered into the world, and death through sin, and so death spread to all men, because all sinned' (*Rom. 5:12*); 'as in Adam all die' (*1 Cor. 15:22*). There are those who say it is not fair that we who live generations after should be penalized for one man's disobedience and folly. Yet, it is universally recognized that the decisions of our parents do affect us. Our political representatives make decisions which affect us also whether we like it or not. The fact is, we are not just an assorted mass of individuals; we belong to families, to our nation, and to the human race. We cannot divorce ourselves from those relationships. Adam stood at the head of the race as our representative and what he did affects us. It was more than just a simple act, however. The scriptures teach that 'when God had created man, *he entered into a covenant of life with him*, upon condition of perfect obedience . . .' (my emphasis).[1] That covenant was made with Adam, 'not only for himself, but for his posterity'.

Question and Answer 18 in The Shorter Catechism unfold this biblical teaching in a helpful way. Question 18 asks: 'Wherein consists the sinfulness of that estate whereinto man fell?' The answer is:

The sinfulness of that estate whereinto man fell, consists in the guilt of Adam's first sin, the want of original righteousness, and the corruption of his whole nature, which is commonly called Original Sin; together with all actual transgressions which proceed from it.

Consider what is involved:

1. There is 'the guilt of Adam's first sin'. Our legal system

---

[1] *Ibid.*, Question 12.

recognizes that an accomplice or partner in crime shares in the guilt. Because a covenant was made with Adam for 'all his posterity', we share his guilt in rebellion against God. Guilt arises when there is a violation of law. Adam knew the command of God, but he deliberately broke it. What he had done contradicted what he knew, and, realizing his guilt, he tried to hide himself from God. We carry that same sense of guilt. We do not need to teach a child how to be embarrassed or filled with shame when he has done what he knows to be wrong. Nor do we need to teach him how to argue his way out of situations; he will try to rationalize his guilt, just as Adam did. The point I want to make, however, is that guilt arises when what we do does not coincide with what we know. While guilt touches the emotions, it begins with *knowledge*.

2. There is 'the want [lack] of original righteousness, and the corruption of [the] whole nature'. Righteousness and corruption are moral matters. They deal with our *character*, what we are. As we shall see, there is no 'divine spark within us'. There is no desire for goodness, because we are corrupt.

3. There are 'actual transgressions'. This term obviously relates to what we *do*. We transgress because we are corrupt in nature, because we lack original righteousness. We can never emphasize too often that we are not sinners because we sin; we sin because we are sinners. Again, we are dealing with the whole man: as he thinks, as he feels, and as he chooses and acts. But, how does this question of sin work out in practical terms? How has sin affected our minds, our morals, and our manners?

I. THE EFFECT OF SIN ON THE MIND

My oldest son is in the U.S. Air Force and has served his first term in working with computers in the Pentagon. On one of my visits to Washington, he was able to get me a security clearance into the place where he worked. The only way I can describe my impression of that vast computer center is to say that I was overwhelmed by the vast reservoir of information. When he told me that each disc contained 2.8 billion pieces of information and that there were literally thousands of discs, I must confess I didn't realize there was that much information to know! It appears as though twentieth-century man is on the verge of omniscience. All that information is stored and is available for instant recall. It appears as though it is only a matter of time before all the gaps in our knowledge will be filled and the deficiencies in our learning rectified. In the light of this, the Bible appears almost obsolete and archaic when it describes man as ignorant and foolish. But then, that is what the scripture says about sinful men: they are 'darkened in their understanding . . . because of the ignorance that is in them' (*Eph. 4:18*). It states also that men, 'professing to be wise, . . . became fools' (*Rom. 1:22*).

The Bible does not deny that sinful men know things; indeed, it says that in the last days 'knowledge will increase' (*Dan. 12:4*). We have, however, at least two major problems:

1. As sinners, we operate within the wrong framework. Think of the field of knowledge as a wagon wheel; each spoke represents a different discipline of study. For the wheel to be useful, it must be properly assembled with the spokes radiating from the hub. You may have seen some of those old Western movies where the wagon wheel falls to pieces. As it hurtles off through the sage brush, spokes fly everywhere. When God is removed as the hub of knowledge, the unifying factor is gone and knowledge disintegrates. That is exactly what has happened; men have removed God from the center of their knowledge and their understanding of the universe has fragmented. God says a man is a fool who says, 'No God!', literally, 'No God for me!' (*Ps. 14:1*). On the other hand, God says, 'The fear of the Lord is the beginning of knowledge' (*Prov. 1:7*). All things must be related to God if they are to be seen in their proper perspective.

Modern education had its roots in Christianity; a great motivation to study both the universe and man grew out of the Christian perspective as a result of the Protestant Reformation. Men realized anew that they lived in God's universe, and they sought to know more about it. For many years after the Reformation, all education was God-centered. Indeed, until recent times, one requirement for graduation from the Universities of Oxford and Cambridge in Great Britain was subscription to the Thirty-nine Articles of the Church of England. Of course, this requirement had become a mere formality by then, but it shows the context out of which education had grown following the

Reformation. In our day, God is almost completely ignored and excluded from our academic institutions, and the results are disturbing. Not only has such exclusion led to the fragmentation of knowledge (disciplines no longer are considered to be concordant or harmonious; truth is no longer a unity); it has led also to lack of direction. As Francis Schaeffer has so capably demonstrated in his lectures, we learn because we have the habit of learning. The motivation is gone. Martin Luther commented, 'If we ever leave God out of our educational structure, our schools will become the hot-beds of hell.' How prophetic! We are reaping the fruit of knowledge without God; the spokes are out of the wheel, flying in all directions as man has lost the only true perspective.

2. The second problem concerns the use of knowledge. Whenever man removes God from the center of his thinking and puts himself at the center of his world, he becomes arrogant and intolerant. The most bigoted people are often those who claim to be liberal. Christian education has generally produced a far better product than the secular institutions, but, in spite of achievements and statistics, this fact is not admitted by secular academics. Indeed, many secular educators despise Christian education and will use all kinds of derogatory terms to describe it. Why? Because Christian education demands that God be central to all things. Sinful man will not recognize that. In other words, the attitude is wrong.

Because man becomes arrogant and intolerant, he cannot be trusted with the knowledge he obtains. For example, we have learned how to process uranium but, as everyone knows and fears, sooner or later that knowledge will be used for wrong ends. (Incidentally, to whom would you entrust an atomic bomb? A man who fears God and lives by the principles of God's word, or an unprincipled and arrogant individual who is intoxicated with his own importance?) Similarly, the problems of ecology, economics, and society stem from men with enough knowledge and selfish motives to make them dangerous. Give a sinful man enough knowledge, and he will cheat on his income tax, defraud others, exploit the environment, and enslave his fellow man. When man gets knowledge out of its proper framework, he cannot be trusted with it.

The Bible is very much up to date when it says that 'the fear of the Lord is the beginning of knowledge, and of wisdom'. Scripture is up to date when it describes men as 'ignorant' and 'darkened in their understanding' (*Eph. 4:18*).

Men have not only forgotten the *context* of true knowledge; they have forgotten the *content*. Listen to conversation in an office or workshop; it consists mostly of sex, boasting, and complaints against the boss or the government. Sinners do not know how to employ their minds in things that are lovely and of good report. They employ their minds in vain and unprofitable things; that is why television programs are unacceptable to the public unless they contain illicit sex and violence. These are the things the unregenerate mind likes to feed on.

A discussion of what is generally called 'mental sickness' is really outside the scope of our study. Let me say, however, that, apart from chemically induced or physical malfunction, there is usually nothing wrong with men's minds. What happens is that the mind functions very well. It comes up with the solution of a false façade to escape problems. It is noteworthy that with the increase of knowledge there has come an alarming increase in 'mental' problems. It is estimated that at the beginning of 1982 there were about 6½ million 'mental' cases in the United States. That is four times as many as there had been twenty-two years previously. This is the fruit of sin. Sin has affected the *mind*.

II. THE EFFECT OF SIN ON THE MORALS

As one observes the sincere concern people show for others and considers the many philanthropic and humanitarian organizations which exist to express that concern, it would appear as though man is not devoid of righteousness. When there are needs within our society, some people give themselves and their resources quite generously. Consequently, we are often impressed and comment, 'He did it out of the generosity and goodness of his heart.' Surely, such generosity must proceed from a good character!

The Bible tells us that 'the heart is more deceitful than all else and is desperately sick; who can understand it?' (*Jer. 17:9*). Secular psychologists confirm this, though they refuse to talk about sin. Consider this comment by a psychologist at the

30

University of Illinois: 'Every person, man or child, spends twenty-four hours a day satisfying or attempting to satisfy his physical, social, and personality needs.'[1] What he is saying is that we spend every moment of every day taking care of ourselves. The world says it even more bluntly, 'You have to take care of Number One!' The reason people help others is because, in some way, it is a personal advantage to do so. Often many kind and generous actions are done, not because of the goodness of the heart, but because the giver wants people to think of him as good and generous. He wants to give the impression that he is righteous.

John Dewey said, 'Christianity will never work because it demands things which are contrary to human nature.' He understood the issue very clearly. Human nature is selfish. Of course, when we talk about righteousness and holiness, we always like to shift the focus from what we *are* to what we *do*. We can do lots of things for the wrong reasons; it is not the act but the motivation behind the act that we must consider. When we do something to impress others, the act might be good, but the motivation is wrong. Being righteous does not depend upon *doing* right; it depends on *being* right.

Because we measure our righteousness by what we do, we tend to use others as our standard. If I do something more than my neighbor, I congratulate myself that I am more righteous than he is. So then, the problem is two-fold: I not only focus on what I have done, but I use the wrong standard. As we have seen previously, the only adequate standard for righteousness and holiness is the character of God. I am required to be perfect as he is perfect. As one of the Puritans said, 'God's righteousness is that righteousness which God's righteousness requires him to require.' We do not start life innocent, or good, or even neutral. We are born with a corrupt nature, and we lack original righteousness.

Jesus said, 'A good tree cannot produce bad fruit, nor can a rotten tree produce good fruit' (*Matt. 7:18*). The Pharisees were what we would have to describe as very good men; they were meticulous in doing good deeds. But, as Jesus pointed out, those deeds were done to be seen of men. He went on to say, 'unless your righteousness surpasses that of the scribes and Pharisees, you shall

[1]Glenn Myers Blair, R. Stewart Jones and Ray H. Simpson, *Educational Psychology* (New York, Macmillan, 1959), p. 327.

not enter the kingdom of heaven' (*Matt. 5:20*). Of course, we need to consider the other side of the coin also. A corrupt tree brings forth bad fruit. Because we have a corrupt nature, 'there is none righteous, not even one' (*Rom. 3:10*). Adam's fall affected our character, our moral nature. Sin has affected what we are and what we desire.

III. THE EFFECT OF SIN ON OUR MANNERS

With all the scientific and technological advancements of this century, it appears as though man still has dominion over the creation. Men have walked on the face of the moon, harnessed the power of the atom, and developed systems of communication hitherto unknown; surely man is master of creation. Yet, while we are able to analyze, synthesize, and utilize the resources of creation, something is radically wrong with our control over nature. The more we have learned and applied technology, the more we have abused, exploited, and polluted the world in which God has placed us.

Such abuse is not really surprising, considering the facts of man's thinking and character. Because man is self-centered, he is greedy. All of us, as sinners, are interested only in the satisfaction of our own needs. Consequently, we exploit and manipulate natural and human resources in order to get all we can out of them. We are not good stewards of the creation entrusted to our care; we do not fulfill the purpose for which God has made us.

There are all kinds of protests, exhortations, and proposed legislation to try to rectify the problem. No matter how much we challenge men to leave some resources for future generations, ultimately such challenges will fall upon deaf ears. The reason is that our concern is for ourselves, not future generations. We have told ourselves that we 'go around only once', and had better make the most of it while we can. Romans chapter 6 makes clear that we are under the dominion of sin, or, as Peter phrases it, we are 'slaves of corruption' (*2 Pet. 2:19*). Instead of exercising dominion, we are slaves.

Adam was made a free and responsible being. The entry of sin did not remove the responsibility, but it brought him (and us) into spiritual bondage. Since Adam, all men have been unable to operate as they ought; they have 'followed the ways of this world and of the ruler of the kingdom of the air, the spirit who is now at work in those who are disobedient' (*Eph. 2:2 NIV*). That condition never changes, not even a second! Many Christians do not understand the nature of our spiritual bondage; there are those who talk a great deal about man's free will. It is true that we are free to do as we please, but the problem is, *what* do we please? We are in bondage to the world, the devil, and the flesh; they dictate our behavior. Because we are 'slaves of corruption', we cannot choose good. The will of man is enslaved by sin; it is therefore incapable of doing the will of God. Man's will is gripped by a bondage which affects everything he does. It affects the way we do oil exploration, use nuclear power, and do our shopping. As one of the Puritans prayed, 'My faculties have been a weapon of revolt against thee; as a rebel I have misused my strength, and served the foul adversary of thy kingdom.'[1]

So then, the fall of Adam has affected our thinking. It has affected our character. And it has affected our will. It has had a total effect. Perhaps the greatest tragedy of all is that we are ignorant of the truth about ourselves. We pride ourselves in our wisdom, our goodness, and our freedom. We are lost and do not know it. That is our predicament. If we are to be saved from this awful condition, it will require nothing less than the power of God. We are not through with the discussion of sin yet, however. Before we can turn to God's great plan of salvation, we will consider what sinful man does to *solve* his problem and what he does to *avoid* his problem. His solutions and rationalizations are truly ingenious; no stone is left unturned. But then, such is the nature of sin; rather than face it, confess it, and forsake it, man seeks to handle it in his own way.

---

[1] *The Valley of Vision*, ed. Arthur Bennett (Edinburgh, Banner of Truth Trust, 1975), p. 70.

Man as God made him	He is a (Faculty)	What Adam did	Sinfulness consists of	What man is because of Adam's sin
Knowledge	Rational being (Mind)	Exchanged the truth of God for a lie	The guilt of Adam's first sin	Darkened in his understanding . . . ignorant
Righteousness & Holiness	Moral being (Desires)	Followed the way which seems right	The want of righteousness; corruption of nature	None righteous, no not one
Dominion	Being with purpose (Will)	Set at nought dominion	Actual transgressions	Under the dominion of sin; a slave of corruption

4: *What Man Does to Solve His Sin Problem*

Following a lecture I gave at the Inter-Varsity chapter of the University of Adelaide in South Australia several years ago, an agnostic student challenged my claim that the Bible is absolute truth. He said it is detrimental (and arrogant) to claim that one has the truth because, when a person makes that claim, he ceases to search. And when we cease to search, we stagnate. He pointed out that while we are searching, we are progressing. We would certainly agree with the television advertisement which says, 'A mind is a terrible thing to waste.' And we would agree with that student that there are few things worse than a stagnant mind. Unfortunately, we have to agree that what he said has some basis, for all too frequently we prefer to settle into a comfortable corner where we do not have to wrestle with problems or think through issues. It is much more convenient to let someone else do our thinking for us, especially in politics and religion.

We, as Christians, certainly claim to possess the truth. However, that does not mean we can be mentally lazy. When we say that the Bible is truth, we do not mean that it is exhaustive (i.e. that it says everything that could be said); we mean that it is accurate in all the statements it does make. Because it is not exhaustive, it provides a base from which to work. The Bible, however, is not simply a book of truth, it is a book of principles. Consequently, we have to think hard to determine the principles and to see how they apply to our daily lives. As someone has said, 'All Christians should be deep thinkers because they are the only ones who have deep things to think about.' The point is that we have a base from which to work and upon which we can build. I pointed out to that student that he was on a journey, but that he had no starting point

35

and had lost sight of the destination. He was engaged in a search that ultimately had no purpose.

Too often it is the ungodly who discover things because of their search. It is interesting to note that the descendants of Cain were the ones who first became skilled in the arts and science (*Gen. 4*). Wickedness and creativity often seem to go together. Apparently, Cain's descendants were searching; they explored alternatives. The scriptures say that 'the wicked are like the tossing sea, for it cannot be quiet' (*Isa. 57:20*), and while that restlessness exists, men keep on searching for something to bring peace and satisfaction to the soul. As Augustine said, 'Our hearts are restless until they find their rest in thee.'

In our studies so far, we have seen that we are made in the image of God in knowledge, but through the fall, we are darkened in understanding. We have been made in God's image in righteousness and holiness but, through the fall, we 'lack original righteousness' and possess 'a corrupt nature'. We have seen also that although we were made 'to exercise dominion', sin has brought us into a condition of spiritual bondage and slavery. Because of our condition, it is impossible to rest. We can never be content in sin. Sin is really a contradiction to our being; we were not made for sin. Sin creates a vacuum; it produces emptiness, discontent, and dissatisfaction. We have explored and continue to explore every conceivable alternative in order to find a solution to our emptiness. We turn, therefore, to consider what we *do* because of what we *are*. What do men do to solve their sin problem?

I. WHAT MEN DO TO SOLVE THEIR INTELLECTUAL NEED

Ultimately, the thirst for knowledge is generated by an intense desire to find meaning and significance in life; we must find the key which will unlock the mystery of our existence and bring us fulfillment and satisfaction. For centuries, philosophers have debated the issues of life, but without success. When the apostle Paul went to Mars Hill in Athens, the philosophers were looking for some new thing; they had evidently exhausted all the possibilities. Modern philosophy plows the same ground without any progress. In fact, it has come to the place where many believe there are no answers and we must die in despair.

While the philosophers have speculated, the scientists have probed the physical and material universe. They have explored the heavens and investigated the atom. They have searched the face of the earth for fossils and researched enzymes in the hope of finding something to give life explanation and meaning. They have studied genetics, the behavior of rats and monkeys, and the submergence habits of the hippopotamus, but none of these things has yielded the answer.

Artists have tried to express the meaning of life on canvas and in music, but their efforts, especially in recent times, have left us not only without an answer but also without art and music. The answers to life are so evasive that modern men have declared the search for meaning in life to be futile and adopted an irrational approach to life. For this reason, many have turned to promiscuity, drugs, and even suicide. I met a brilliant British scientist in Switzerland some years ago who took his research seriously. He believed, however, that the best thing that could happen is for the ice caps to melt and destroy the human race. Many modern men have given up all hope of finding a rational solution to life. And yet, we cannot be satisfied with an irrational solution any more than we can be with no solution.

Daniel, the prophet, informs us that in the end times men 'shall run to and fro, and knowledge shall be increased' (*Dan. 12:4 KJV*). Paul speaks in similar terms: 'in the last days . . . men will be . . . always learning and never able to come to the knowledge of the truth' (*2 Tim. 3:1–7*). If men are ever learning, why is it impossible for them to come to the knowledge of the truth? Within this passage, Paul gives a list of things which will characterize men in the last days. It would be profitable, of course, to examine the entire list, but notice three which stand out. 'Men will be lovers of self' (*v. 2*), 'lovers of money' (*v. 2*), and 'lovers of pleasure' (*v. 4*). One primary reason why we 'ever learn but do not come to the knowledge of the truth' is because we learn in terms of self, money, and pleasure. One has only to listen to the news any day to see that the things which interest us are those things which have a direct bearing on our earthly lives, our economy, and our pleasure. As I have said previously, we have the wrong reference point (ourselves) and we have the wrong framework (self, money, and pleasure).

In the previous chapter, 2 Timothy chapter 2, the King James Version uses an intriguing phrase to describe the condition of men. It speaks of them as 'those that oppose themselves' (v. 25). Most modern translations tend to miss the point of this statement; I believe the apostle is conveying the idea that men work against themselves, against their own interests. Bernard translates it as 'those who are adversely affected'.[1] Because men work against themselves, 'the Lord's bond-servant must . . . [be] able to teach' (v. 24). Why teach? 'Perhaps God may grant them repentance leading to the knowledge of the truth,' and (as the NIV says) 'they will come to their senses and escape from the trap of the devil' (v. 26). Paul says it is impossible for men to come to the knowledge of the truth, because they have been trapped. Though they seek to know the truth, they have been snared into believing that truth concerns self, money, and pleasure. To come to the knowledge of the truth depends upon *repentance*; it depends upon an entirely different approach. While men do 'not see fit to acknowledge God' (*Rom. 1:28*), the search will continue without satisfactory results. We were not made to be ignorant; we cannot rest in ignorance. The search for truth will continue until we turn from our wicked ways and 'seek the Lord while He may be found' (*Isa. 55:6–7*). The key to knowledge is repentance. Instead, to solve our intellectual problem, we 'ever learn'.

II. WHAT MEN DO TO SOLVE THEIR MORAL NEED

The scriptures are clear: 'There is none righteous, not even one' (*Rom. 3:10*). Are men aware that they are not righteous? And if they are aware, do they try to do anything about it? If you were to go downtown to a bar or some 'hot' spot and begin to talk to the people there about righteousness and holiness, what do you think their response would be? Probably, they would help you out of the door, giving you a foot start! Are they interested in righteousness? While it might appear otherwise, righteousness is a matter of deep concern to them. It is not uncommon or unusual to hear people of the world express themselves in these terms: 'Sure, I have a few

[1]Donald Guthrie, *The Pastoral Epistles*, Tyndale Bible Commentaries, (Grand Rapids, Eerdmans, 1964), p. 154.

38

beers, and once in a while I have an argument with the missus, but I'm not as bad as my neighbor – and he goes to church.' What that means is that they claim to be righteous, and they are trying to establish their righteousness by using their neighbor as the standard of measurement.

When I was a student at Moody Bible Institute I was assigned to some practical Christian work downtown at one of the rescue missions on 'Skid Row'. Most of the men on 'Skid Row' were utterly derelict; some had lost fingers and toes through frostbite from sleeping in the gutters and on the streets. And most of them were not the only creatures within their ragged clothes! Even among such men, however, there was still an attempt to establish righteousness. Often one would comment, 'I know I'm down, but I'm not as bad as that fellow, and I have been down here on "Skid Row" twice as long as he has.' No doubt, a man can always find someone else with whom he can compare himself. Such comparisons are, of course, utterly futile. Our righteousness and holiness can never be established by comparing ourselves with other sinful men. The standard, as we have seen, is the character of God. 'When they measure themselves by themselves,' says the apostle, 'and compare themselves with themselves, they are without understanding' (2 Cor. 10:12).

Sometimes we attempt to establish our righteousness by appealing to our religious heritage or religious associations. It is interesting to be able to say that one has had personal contact with Billy Graham, met with the archbishop, or had an interview with the Pope, but that is all it is – interesting! Our contact or association with religious leaders does not in any way earn us any merit or make us one whit more righteous. Personally, I can claim a fine religious heritage. The 'Leigh' part of my name goes back to the Rev. Samuel Leigh, one of the successors of John Wesley, who was the first to be sent by the Methodists to Australia to forward the work of the gospel. But while I value that heritage, it does not make me one bit more righteous, though I confess I have used it at times to give that impression.

Under one of the beautiful stained glass windows in one of the cathedrals in Australia there is an inscription telling of a man who migrated to Australia about 1800. It states that he selected (i.e. homesteaded) a large piece of land, prospered, and selected more land. Later in the century he died. And then, a postscript is added. It says he was related to one of the translators of the Bible. That is a sad but rather typical commentary. His wealth made him important in the eyes of men, and his relationship to a preacher was somehow supposed to make him righteous.

Though the apostle Paul is specifically speaking of the Jews, his comment is appropriate to us all. He says, 'they being ignorant of God's righteousness, and going about to establish their own righteousness, have not submitted themselves to the righteousness of God' (*Rom. 10:3 KJV*). Man was not made to be unrighteous and unholy; we cannot rest in sin and unrighteousness. We can never be satisfied while we are less than we should be. We can never be content with our moral condition; hence, we endeavor to establish our own righteousness.

III. WHAT MEN DO TO SOLVE THEIR
NEED FOR PURPOSE

Men have always been restless and discontented, it seems. It is doubtful, however, if that discontent has ever been more visibly evident than in the twentieth century. In the Western world, at least, we have had more things, more leisure, more entertainment, more opportunities for work, and more freedom than any previous generation. Many have tried to find the answers through learning, only to discover that 'increasing knowledge results in increasing pain' (*Eccles. 1:18*). Others have tried to find fulfillment and purpose in the accumulation of material things and personal wealth, but they too discover that they are 'striving after wind' (*Eccles. 2:11*). Still others have given themselves to the pursuit of pleasure, only to find that they are soon drained of their youthful vitality and their souls are still empty.

All kinds of efforts are being made in these days to create the perfect society. It is argued that if the civil rights of all men can be guaranteed, we will enjoy unrestricted freedom. When the lot of the oppressed minorities is improved, and we all have equal opportunity and equal wealth and proper government legislation, then, surely, all the problems will be solved. At least, that is the hope. Sad to say, this kind of thinking is evident even in the church. Men have always been fascinated by the promise of utopia, the perfect world. The current concept is radical; it calls for the overthrow of the 'establishment'. Actually, that is quite an admission: it is saying that all past efforts have failed, and that to get what we want, we must begin with a clean slate. Such a concept is an admission that all men are in bondage and must be set free. The promise of freedom gives the movement impetus.

As an expression of the need for freedom, the revolutionary and the black man raise clenched fists, and women march in protest for their rights and liberation. I do not deny the black man his rights, but I would hasten to say that it is not only the black man who is bound, nor only the revolutionary who is enslaved. Indeed, women need to be liberated, but so do men! As we saw in our last study, *all* men are slaves of corruption; we are all under the bondage of sin. We may applaud the efforts of William Wilberforce and Abraham Lincoln to abolish slavery. They dealt with physical slavery. The enslavement of the body, bad though that might be (although we generally tend to think in terms of the abuses), is preferable to the enslavement of the soul. Our modern world has become acutely aware that our bondage is of a spiritual nature, and multitudes are prepared to fight to be free.

The comment of the apostle Peter is appropriate; he says, 'promising them freedom while they themselves are slaves of corruption' (*2 Pet. 2:19*). The problem is, of course, that slaves cannot free themselves. The promise of freedom is hollow and empty. We must first recognize the true nature of our problem. Until we realize that we have been made by God for a purpose, we shall remain discontented and restless. Even if the 'establishment' is overthrown, the cry for freedom will still be with us.

In spite of the unceasing efforts to solve the problems of sin and to find purpose and meaning for our existence, we are no closer to a solution than the first son of Adam. We have turned every stone without finding the desired result. Finding the solution will require more than a brilliant mind; it will take more than self-righteous effort; it will take more than a revolutionary promise of freedom. The solution to sin requires the wisdom, grace, and power of God.

Man as God made him	What Adam did	What man is	What man does to solve his sin problem*
Knowledge	Exchanged God's truth <u>Mind set</u> against truth	Darkened in his understanding . . . ignorant (*Eph. 4:18*)	Ever learning but never able to come to knowledge of truth (*2 Tim. 3:7*)
Righteousness & Holiness	Exchanged God's character <u>Desires set</u> against right	None righteous, no not one (*Rom. 3:10*)	Seeks to establish his own righteousness (*Rom. 10:3*)
Dominion	Exchanged God's purpose <u>Will set against</u> God's will	Under dominion of sin (*Rom. 6*) Slaves of corruption (*2 Pet. 2:19*)	Promises freedom (*2 Pet. 2:19*)

5: *What Man Does to Avoid His Sin Problem*

Suppose you went out to your garage one morning only to discover that your car would not start. You do not know it, but you have problems in the carburation, in the ignition, and in the transmission. Your car is getting no gas, and even if it did, there is no spark to ignite it. In addition to that, even if you could get the engine running, it still would not move. With problems like that you would probably call the junk yard and tell them to come and get it. However, you restrain yourself; instead, you call a mechanic. The mechanic stands back, looks it over, and declares, 'That's a pretty nice car you have there; it looks as if it is in really good shape.' Well, you try to convince him that something is wrong, so finally he brings out his diagnostic equipment and begins to check the car throughout. He discovers that the points have a gap ten times more than the book specifies. He finds that the firing order is just the opposite of what it should be and that the timing is fifty degrees off. As you watch, you think to yourself, 'At least we are getting somewhere; we know some of the problems.' But, to your consternation, instead of going to work on your car, the mechanic takes out his pen and begins to change the manufacturer's specifications to agree with your car. He then proceeds to tell you that there is really nothing wrong; the manufacturer really did not know what he was doing and the problem was in the manual.

That would be serious enough in dealing with a car. What would we have to say about a doctor who examined a patient with a terminal illness and began to change his medical books to correspond to the patient's condition? We simply would not tolerate that kind of thing when it comes to our physical well-being. Sad to say, when it comes to our souls, we respect and honor the man who operates that way. Philosophers and educators (who,

43

in a general way, deal with the mind), ministers (who supposedly deal with morals), and psychiatrists and psychologists (who are supposed to be experts in man's behavior) are often respected and honored in our society but, instead of correcting the man, they often try to adjust and 'correct' the Maker's manual. We have the Maker's manual; in it, we learn what a normal human being is supposed to be like. In it we learn what corrections and adjustments must be made within us to make us correspond to the Maker's specifications. But rather than face the problem, we try to correct the manual! We rationalize our problems, excuse them, evade them, minimize them, and avoid them.

Of course, it is difficult, if not impossible, to deny that there is something wrong. The alternative is, of course, to focus upon the ignition and forget about the carburation and transmission. We would like to convince ourselves that sin has not had a total effect. And, as we have seen previously, if the effect has not been total, the possibility exists for us to help ourselves out of our predicament. We have seen already, however, that sin has affected the whole man; it has affected the mind, the desires, and the will. Yet, in spite of the evidence, we are not ready to accept the verdict; we will not accept the diagnosis of the Great Physician. Since men have not been able to solve the problem by 'ever learning', by 'seeking to establish their own righteousness', and by 'promising freedom', they think the next best thing to do is to explain it, to deny it, to avoid it. I hope our general consideration will help us to see how serious the problem really is.

I. RATIONALISTIC ARGUMENTS TO AVOID
THE SIN PROBLEM

Knowledge is like the fuel in the tank of our car; we operate on knowledge. In one sense, we can say that the more we put into the tank, the further we go. But, the problem is, an enemy has come and put sugar in the tank. Sugar is sweet to the taste but, mixed with gasoline, it will only gum up the carburation system. As we have seen previously, the sweet lie of Satan has polluted our minds; we are prejudiced against the truth, and we have the wrong framework for our thinking. It might appear to be pure, but when polluted with Satan's lie, knowledge is destructive; we cannot operate on it properly.

In spite of this, we go to great lengths to avoid the problem. As sinners, we operate as though our thinking is infallible and our reasoning impeccable. We ignore our problem with spiritual carburation. We begin with the premise that our minds are the highest and final authority in all matters. Consequently, when our minds come into conflict with the Maker's manual, rather than correcting our thinking, we 'correct' the manual.

Recently, I heard a preacher on the radio say that we only confuse the young people in our churches when we teach them creation. Creation is not compatible, it is said, with modern scientific data; therefore, the teaching of creation is archaic – even though science has not yet said the last word on the origin of things! Being unable to explain the Bible, especially the miracles and the life of Jesus Christ, in terms of naturalistic science, many modern theologians have affirmed that religious faith is irrational and absurd. We believe, they say, in spite of the evidence. But God's word *is* reasonable; the problem is that there is sugar in the tank! Because men consider their minds to be the ultimate authority in all matters, they consider themselves able to stand in judgment of what God has said.

Rationalism takes two forms in relation to God's word. The first form acknowledges the Bible to be the word of God but denies its sufficiency. For example, the Pharisees believed that the Bible was a divine revelation but that it was not adequate as a guide for practical daily living. They devised, therefore, a multitude of legalistic requirements to cover every specific situation and detail of life. Through additions, they sought to make the Bible sufficient. Naturally, this produced a legalistic system; if a person did what the Pharisees required, he was, in their opinion, right with God. They rejected Jesus because he did not fit into their system. It was the mind of man which specified what was required and determined whether the requirement had been met. The mind of man took precedence over the word of God.

The same mentality existed among the Judaizers who insisted that circumcision be added to the gospel. The apostle Paul wrote the Epistle to the Galatians to refute that error and to establish the fact that the gospel alone is sufficient. The Judaizers had decided that what God was saying in the gospel was inadequate and insufficient.

45

I regret to say that much of the so-called charismatic movement of our day falls into the same grievous error; it adds to the gospel and makes requirements beyond the gospel. Similarly, there are those who affirm that the Bible is inerrant in matters of faith and practice, but not in science and history. This is another subtle way of declaring that the word of God is not sufficient and must bow before the 'assured conclusions' of men.

A second form of rationalism denies the Bible as the word of God. Those who deny its *sufficiency* insist on *additions*; those who deny its *authority* make *substitutions*. Paul also engaged in controversy with a form of Gnostic teaching that claimed superior knowledge to what was in the Bible. A decisive answer to this error is given in the Book of Colossians, where we are told that in Christ 'are hidden all the treasures of wisdom and knowledge' (*Col. 2:3*). Modern gnostics are not difficult to find; many theological seminaries world-wide (not all, thank God!) are dominated by men who build their theology upon the philosophy and psychology of men rather than on the word of God. And, of course, such modern gnosticism takes many different shapes and forms.

Whenever the Bible is abandoned as the authority, an alternative must be found. That alternative is some form of rationalism or mysticism. Modern-day gnostics must find another *revelation* (as, for example, *The Book of Mormon*) or they must find another *explanation*. And always the results are tragic. Permit me to give one example. Thomas Aquinas (*1225?–74*), the great theologian of the Roman Catholic Church, systematized his theology on the basis of Greek thought rather than exclusively on the Bible. He adopted a rationalistic approach. When such intellectual rationalism influenced *the pulpit*, the common man was overwhelmed with the lofty thoughts of Greek philosophy, and, more and more, he retreated. Naturally, he thought the clergy knew what they were talking about, but he could not keep up with it. Consequently, he found it necessary to let the Church think and act for him. I believe that this opened the door for the doctrine of papal infallibility. When there is a religious élite who do the thinking for the people, the ordinary man abandons conviction and submits to whatever edicts are delivered to him. Even today, Roman Catholics will admit that they let the Church decide all religious issues.

That happened in the Roman Catholic Church; it is happening in modern Protestantism also. In different ways, the word of God is liable to be replaced by the philosophical speculations of such men as Karl Barth, Paul Tillich, Rudolph Bultmann, and even Herman Dooyeweerd. As we might expect, this is producing a religious élite who interpret, determine, and dictate what men are to believe and how they are to behave. More and more, the man in the pew is abandoning conviction to let the church think for him. It is ironic that rationalistic approaches actually plunge men deeper into intellectual and spiritual darkness.

God's word is the ultimate authority. Humbly, we must accept his diagnosis. We must take him at his word. Sin has affected the mind, not only in giving us the wrong context and content, not only in prejudicing us against the truth, but in making us think we are superior to God. We cannot avoid the effect of sin so easily, however. Rational arguments will never enable us to evade the issue.

II. MORALISTIC ARGUMENTS TO AVOID
THE SIN PROBLEM

If knowledge is like the carburation in your car, the desires of the heart must be like the ignition. To function properly, the spark must be distributed evenly. The desires of the heart must be directed and controlled. Because of sin, the desires of man are always short-circuiting. In spite of the biblical testimony about our moral condition and desires, many efforts have been made to correct the Maker's manual in this area also. It is not at all uncommon to hear people speak about man being basically good. In the last century, Schleiermacher built a whole system of theology around the 'divine spark' within us. It was not biblical, of course, but a moralistic attempt to avoid the sin problem.

In order to avoid the biblical facts about our moral condition, it is usually necessary to deny or re-define sin. There are those who teach a doctrine of 'sinless perfection' or 'entire sanctification'. To establish this doctrine, they find it necessary to make the distinction between 'sin' and 'mistakes'. They affirm that a person can be perfect and still make mistakes. If the person sins, however, he not only loses his perfection, but he loses his salvation. Roman Catholicism makes a similar and equally serious mistake by classifying sin as either 'mortal' or 'venial' (i.e. excusable). If sin can be categorized in this way, then our moral condition is not too serious. If we merely make mistakes or commit excusable sins, then much of our personal responsibility is minimized. We are excusable! I have often wondered how those who hold to this position explain the fact that God required sacrifice for sins of ignorance in the Old Testament.

To re-classify sin is a subtle way to avoid the real issue. Though some sins are more serious than others (see the Westminster Larger Catechism, Question 151), the size of the sin is not really the issue. As we have already seen, it is not what we *do* that makes us sinners; it is what we *are*. Again, we are not sinners because we sin; we sin because we are sinners. The attempt to by-pass the moral condition and focus only upon the act merely serves to show how serious the problem really is.

The same problem surfaces in much present-day evangelism. There are many who try to present the gospel in a positive and inoffensive manner. To approach a sinner and to say to him, 'God loves you and has a wonderful plan for your life', is certainly positive and inoffensive, but it fails to deal with the primary issue. To give the impression that a man is acceptable to God without a change of nature is a very serious error. John Wesley understood this. He said, 'One in a thousand may have been awakened by the Gospel: But this is no general rule: The ordinary method of God, is to convict sinners by the Law, and that only.'[1] In other words, there is no gospel to offer until people first see themselves as sinners before an angry God. One cannot help but lament the many emotionally oriented activities these days designed to make people *feel* good instead of giving them the gospel to *make* them good.

Rationalistic attempts to avoid the problem of sin are essentially a declaration that sin has not affected the mind. Moralistic attempts are really a denial that sin has affected the character. We are so skillful at minimizing, evading, or avoiding the issue

[1]John Wesley, *Sermons on Several Occasions* (London, Wesley Conference Office, n.d.), p. 424.

and thereby silencing an uneasy conscience. The Psalmist declared, 'deliverance by man is in vain' (*Ps. 108:12*). As Solomon said, 'He who conceals his transgressions will not prosper, but he who confesses and forsakes them will find compassion' (*Prov. 28:13*). Moralistic arguments will never enable us to conceal our sin.

III. DETERMINISTIC EFFORTS TO AVOID
THE SIN PROBLEM

Perhaps you are wondering why I found so many things wrong with your car in my opening illustration. Well, if the fuel system illustrates the mind and the ignition system the desires, the transmission obviously illustrates the will. I think that many people have never even considered that there could be trouble with the will too. As we have seen already, sin has affected the whole man, and not merely a part of him.

Traditionally, New Year's Eve is the time when we make our resolutions. We determine to change our lives, to give up something we do which is harmful or detrimental to our health or which costs too much money. Sometimes we resolve to be more positive, more thoughtful, more considerate, and more helpful. Alas, in spite of our determined efforts, we soon fall back into our old rut, and nothing has changed. In fact, we don't talk much about resolutions anymore; it is a bit of an embarrassment, and we treat it as a joke. We fail, and then another year comes around; we grit our teeth with even greater determination and say to ourselves, 'This year, I really am going to do it.' Somehow that usually does not work.

The simple fact is we cannot change our lives by determined effort or an act of the will. Jeremiah wrote, 'Can the Ethiopian change his skin or the leopard his spots? Then you also can do good who are accustomed to do evil' (*Jer. 13:23*). In order to understand the problem, we need to see how the will operates. From our everyday experience, it should be evident that every decision we make (i.e. an act of the will) is based on what we *know* and how we *feel*. For example, I am not going to the football game today because:

1. I do not *know* if there is a football game.

2. Even if there were, I have no *desire* to go. (Apologies to football fans!)

Of course, these two aspects are not always in the same proportions; sometimes one is more dominant than the other. During my pastoral ministry, I have had several young ladies come to my office to inform me that they wanted to get married to a man who was not a Christian. Occasionally, they have listened to counsel, but, as often as not, they have responded by saying, 'I know what the Bible says, but I want to do it anyway.' The decision is based upon strong desires. On the other hand, I have had many women come for counseling who have told me, 'If only I had known my husband as I do now, I would never have married him.' What they are saying is that they made a decision without sufficient knowledge. Our decisions are based on what we know and how we feel.

Now, how does this relate to our spiritual life? Recently, I heard a popular evangelist preaching to a television audience. He stated emphatically, 'You can by an act of the will accept Jesus Christ as your Savior.' The way he presented it suggested that the one faculty of man which had escaped the ruinous effect of the fall was the will. He appealed to people to exercise their will as though it possessed some mysterious capacity to deliver us from our sinful predicament. The problem is, of course, that sinful man neither *knows* God nor *desires* God. To invite a sinner to exercise his will in opposition to what he knows and how he feels is to ask him to do the impossible. It is little wonder that so many modern-day 'converts' do not persevere in their profession. Deliverance from sin requires something more than a New Year's resolution or a determined effort. We cannot avoid the problem of sin by ignoring its ruinous effect on the will. Salvation does not depend on the man who *wills* or the man who runs, but on God who has mercy' (*Rom. 9:16*; my emphasis). We are born into God's family not 'of the *will* of the flesh, nor of the *will* of man, but of God' (*John 1:13*; my emphasis).

We can rationalize, moralize, and fantasize, but simplistic solutions which, at some point, place salvation in the hands of men, will not suffice. The car will never function until it is corrected according to the Maker's manual.

One of the Puritans prayed,

When thou wouldst guide me I control myself,
When thou wouldst be sovereign I rule myself.
When thou wouldst take care of me I suffice myself.
When I should depend on thy providings I supply myself,
When I should submit to thy providence I follow my will,
When I should study, love, honour, trust thee, I serve myself;
I fault and correct thy laws to suit myself.[1]

Man as God made him	Effects of sin	What man affirms	Man avoids problem by
Knowledge	Darkened in understanding (*Eph. 4:18*) Mind set against truth	Sin has not affected the mind	Rationalistic arguments
Righteousness & Holiness	Unrighteousness (*Rom. 3:10*) Desires set against right	Sin has not affected the nature (character)	Moralistic arguments
Dominion	Slave of corruption (*2 Pet. 2:19*) Will set against God's will	Sin has not affected the will	Deterministic arguments

[1] *The Valley of Vision*, ed. Arthur Bennett, p. 91.

6: *What Man Needs: The Three 'R's' of Redemption*

When John Dewey introduced his pragmatic philosophy into the educational system of the United States of America, he brought about a radical change. He claimed that education up to that point had been considered as *preparation* for life and was therefore *subject*-oriented; he affirmed that education *is* life and therefore ought to be *student*-oriented. Since Dewey believed that life is made up of problems, he insisted that education should equip children to solve problems pragmatically; that is, whatever works is right. Dewey's philosophy undercut all absolutes; as someone has said, 'The only absolute he had was: "Absolutely no absolutes".' This gave us a new approach to everything; it brought to us the new mathematics, for example. Instead of teaching our children that 2 plus 2 equals 4, they were taught that 2 plus 1 is less than 4. In our day we are beginning to reap the fruit of his philosophy; we have teachers who cannot read, spell, or do simple arithmetic and who object to being tested for their jobs. At any rate, we have developed an educational system which has brought us into deep trouble; popular news magazines carry articles and various analyses about the failure of our schools, but no one seems to have the answers. We have discovered that it is impossible to ignore the 'three R's'. We must get back to the basics. It is impossible to have effective education without the 'three R's'.

Similarly, it is impossible to have effective redemption without the 'three R's'; they too are basic. Let me hasten to say I am not talking about the same 'three R's', but, as we shall see, they are not entirely unrelated. We have been considering the problem of sin. We would prefer to avoid the issue because it is unpleasant and painful, but we cannot. We must understand the nature of our problem if we are to see our need of Christ as our Savior. It should not surprise us to discover that God is so infinitely wise that he has designed the plan of salvation to meet every aspect of our need. It fits exactly.

When Adam sinned, there were both objective and subjective factors involved; that is, sin has external and internal effects. Obviously, if the problem is to be solved, the solution must cover both aspects; it must provide what we need outwardly and transform us inwardly. In this chapter, we shall consider what we need; in subsequent chapters we shall look at how these needs are met. As sinners, what do we need?

I. THE NEED FOR REVELATION AND
RATIONAL TRANSFORMATION

The Psalmist tells us that 'the heavens are telling of the glory of God; and the firmament is declaring the work of His hands' (*Ps. 19:1*). In the New Testament we read, 'since the creation of the world His invisible attributes, His eternal power and divine nature, have been clearly seen, being understood through what has been made' (*Rom. 1:20*). In other words, we cannot observe the creation without being confronted by irrefutable evidence for the existence of God. What we see in creation ought to cause us to bow before God as Creator; it ought to cause us to seek him. Because of the effects of sin, we will not bow before God; for this reason, the scriptures declare that all men 'are without excuse' (*Rom. 1:20*). The information we get from creation provides enough light to condemn us; it does not, however, provide enough light to save us.

Our salvation is not a matter of gathering additional data about the universe in which we live; we have already seen that men are 'always learning and never able to come to the knowledge of the truth' (*2 Tim. 3:7*). We do need more information, however. We need that information which will enable us to put things in their proper perspective; we need the truth which Adam exchanged for a lie. How do we get it? In 1 Corinthians 2:9 we are told that the things of God are not perceived by using the eye, the ear, or the heart. I do not believe that the apostle chose those parts of the body arbitrarily. The eye is used by the scientist to make his observation; the ear is employed by the philosopher as he speculates; and the heart is involved when the artist expresses his feelings in music, drama, or art. No matter how intense and careful our observation, no matter how exact our speculation, and no matter how inspiring our artistic work might be, these things will not yield the information we need.

Where do we get the information we so desperately need? The knowledge we need does not come through using a microscope, a telescope or a stethoscope. I Corinthians chapter 2, tells us that God *reveals* these things to us. The first 'R' of redemption is *revelation*. Though we are rebels – indeed, enemies of God – he has, in his infinite mercy and love, condescended to speak to us and to disclose the information we need. The revelation God has given to us is given in verbal propositions which we can read and understand. In the revelation, God has told us about himself. We learn that he is the Creator and Sustainer of all things. In this book, we discover how all things relate to God; above all, it shows us how we can have a restored relationship to him. The revelation gives to us the information we need in order to have a true perspective and to think accurately. This body of information is the *objective* factor.

Adam, you will remember, not only 'exchanged the truth of God for a lie' (*Rom. 1:25*); he set his mind against the truth. Hence, we need renewed minds also. There must be an inward transformation. Consider what the New Testament says:

Be renewed in the spirit of your mind (*Eph. 4:23*).
Be transformed by the renewing of your mind (*Rom. 12:2*).
Casting down imaginations, and every high thing that exalteth itself
    against the knowledge of God, and bringing into captivity every
    thought to the obedience of Christ (*2 Cor. 10:5 KJV*).
Let this mind be in you, which was also in Christ Jesus (*Phil. 2:5 KJV*).

These verses, and others, show us that there must be a radical change in our thought-life. It is not God's mind which is perverted; it is ours!

The radical change of mind we need will never take place while we feast our minds on perverted philosophy or sensual immorality; our minds are transformed by the word of God. Over three centuries ago, Sir Thomas Browne wrote, 'Make not thy Head a Grave, but a Repository of God's mercies.'[1] To make that our

[1]Sir Thomas Browne, *Religio Medici* (London, Macmillan, 1881), p. 172.

testimony, we must study and meditate on God's word. I said earlier that the 'three R's' of the schoolroom are not far removed from the 'three R's' of redemption; *reading* and *revelation* have an obvious relationship. Your mind will never be transformed if you do not read the revelation.

II. THE NEED FOR RECONCILIATION
AND MORAL TRANSFORMATION

When I was in high school, my father pastored a church in a pretty little Australian town with the alluring name of Poowong. Most of the land around the town was very steep, and it was not always easy to find a place flat enough to build on. The site where the church was built was so steep that the aisle was actually a stairway with every row of pews on a different level. When my father walked down the aisle and then up another set of stairs to get to the pulpit, he was on a level with the back row of pews. To say the least, it was a very unusual building, and the impression of physical separation made communication difficult; it created a definite psychological barrier.

In life we know and experience many kinds of barriers and separations. People are separated by geographical distance, by economic status, by religious difference, by moral standards, and political ideologies. Some of these things create real problems and make it difficult for people to live together in harmony. No separation, however, is as bad as that where an offence has been committed or a wrong done. As Proverbs 18:19 says, 'A brother offended is harder to be won than a strong city, and contentions are like the bars of a castle.' If that is true of an offended brother, what must we say about an offended God? The Catechism says, 'All mankind by their fall lost communion with God, are under his wrath and curse, and so made liable to all miseries in this life, to death itself, and to the pains of hell for ever.'[1] Note the fact that we have 'lost communion with God'. We are separated from God because we have offended him. Further, because we have offended him, we stand 'under his wrath and curse'. In recent years, we have heard so much talk about the love of God that many seem to

[1] The Shorter Catechism, Question 19.

have gained the impression that they can swagger into God's presence whenever they feel like it. Such is not the case; God is offended, and he is angry. Our salvation must include some means to appease his wrath and remove his curse. Somehow, we must be brought back into communion with God. In other words, our salvation must include *reconciliation*. God could have justly condemned us and made us pay for our own sin; he could have washed his hands of us, as it were, and destroyed us. Instead, he sent his Son, who, through his sinless life and atoning death, appeased God's wrath and removed the curse. As John Newton wrote:

> He has washed us with his blood,
> He has brought us nigh to God.[1]

It is essential to have a right relationship with God but that is not all. One of the old Anglican bishops said that there were many people who hoped to go to heaven but would be entirely out of place there. The person who has no desire for holiness and righteousness would be utterly miserable in heaven. In other words, our salvation must include transformation of character. God is righteous and holy, but we, as sinners, are unrighteous and unholy. Righteousness and unrighteousness are like oil and water; they do not mix. We lack original righteousness and we possess a corrupt nature; unless we are changed inwardly, we cannot dwell in God's presence. As we have seen previously, we cannot establish our own righteousness by comparing ourselves with others, by diligent and consistent religious ritual or penance, by human resolution or legislation, or by positive thinking. God says, 'Although you wash yourself with lye and use much soap, the stain of your iniquity is before Me' (*Jer. 2:22*). God has sent his Son, not only to reconcile us to God but to transform us. 'If any man is in Christ, he is a new creature; the old things passed away; behold, new things have come' (*2 Cor. 5:17*).

To the objective factors, revelation and reconciliation, nothing needs to be added; they are complete. In the subjective aspects, however, we must 'grow in grace and knowledge'. The change of

---

[1] *Trinity Hymnal* (Philadelphia, Orthodox Presbyterian Church, 1961), Hymn 127: 'Let us love, and sing, and wonder'.

mind and desires is continual until we are ushered into the presence of God. There must be continual growth and development. If there is no desire for the things of God, we need to examine ourselves to make our 'calling and election sure'.

III. THE NEED FOR RESTORATION AND TRANSFORMATION OF THE WILL

The educational system in the state of Victoria (Australia) where I grew up required six years of grade school for the mastering of the 'three R's' and then two, four, or six more years in high school, depending on what the student wanted to do. After the eighth year a major decision had to be made. The student could drop out of school and begin to work as an apprentice for a tradesman or, if he continued in school, he had to decide whether he wanted to pursue a professional, a commercial, or a technical vocation. Fortunately, the system is not so rigid any more. The old system placed the child under tremendous pressure, and, as often as not, he was pushed by his parents into an area for which he was unsuited and in which he had no particular interest.

In these days the choices are so varied, and occupations change so rapidly, that many young people in college find it difficult to decide what they want to do. Some have to settle for whatever work they can find and, of course, some prefer not to work at all. Relatively few, it seems, find their 'niche' and are enthusiastic about their occupation. Generally, people consider themselves fortunate to find a position which offers security, a good salary, opportunity for advancement, and good fringe benefits. If they can have those things they are prepared to put in the necessary hours at the job. They look forward to five o'clock on Friday when they can escape from the drudgery of work for a pleasant weekend. With the prevailing attitude towards work, it is no wonder that so many are restless and discontented.

When a couple come to me for marriage counseling, I begin by asking them why they want to get married. Well, the answer is almost always the same: 'Because we love one another.' Love is important, of course, but usually they are quite surprised when I tell them that that is not where we must start. A marriage based on romantic notions or feelings does not have an adequate base. In

Genesis 2:18 God says, 'It is not good for the man to be alone; I will make him a helper suitable for him.' God makes a man with particular gifts for a particular purpose. Then he calls a woman alongside that man to enable him to fulfill the purpose. There is more to marriage unity than the physical relationship. The problem today is that too many men work simply because they have to have a job; they drift through life. The man has no real sense of calling or purpose, and because of his disinterestedness, the wife is not involved. She decides that she might as well get a job too, and she drifts in another direction. Generally, it is God's plan that a man determine what God wants him to do, and then he gives him a wife to help him do it; that is, together they fulfill a purpose.

But now what do work and marriage have to do with salvation? Sad to say, many people never bring these matters together in their thinking. Salvation is not merely a ticket to heaven when this life is done; salvation does not mean just living a good moral life. Jesus came to give us life and to give it to us abundantly (*John 10:10*); if we drift through our work day by day without purpose and merely tolerate marriage, surely something is wrong. Salvation is not affecting our daily lives.

When the Israelites were in Egyptian bondage, they cried out for deliverance and freedom. They were slaves; they knew what drudgery and monotony were. They could cry out as loudly as they pleased, but it was futile while they were held by the Egyptian taskmasters. They realized that they were not able to function freely and fulfill the purpose for which they had been made. The Egyptians did their thinking for them and the Israelites simply did what they were told to do. The difference between them and the modern worker is not very great. What the Israelites needed, of course, was a deliverer, someone who would rescue them from the hand of the Egyptians and set them free. They needed *restoration* so that they could fulfill the purpose for which God had made them.

Furthermore, when God sent Moses to deliver the Israelites, they could not handle the situation. When they arrived in the wilderness, they had to depend upon God and think for themselves. Many of them became concerned and wanted to return to Egypt where they could eat cucumbers, leeks and garlic to the full (I never could understand that!). When we are in sin, we do not depend on God, nor do we really have to think for ourselves. The world will tell us what we have to do to get a job and why we should get one; it will tell us what to look for and what to expect. The world will tell us how to find a partner; it will tell us what to look for and what to expect there too. The world dictates the terms, and if things do not work out well, it replies, 'That's the way the ball bounces.' Instead of depending on God and thinking for themselves, many people would prefer to remain in 'Egypt'; life there involves bondage but it is secure.

God has sent his Deliverer; he has 'disarmed the rulers and authorities' and set his people free (*Col. 2:15*). The Psalmist says, 'He brought me up out of the pit of destruction, out of the miry clay; and He set my feet upon a rock, making my footsteps firm' (*Ps. 40:2*). 'It was for freedom that Christ set us free' (*Gal. 5:1*). But Christ did not come only to rescue us from the bondage of sin; he came to restore us to a meaningful and fruitful life, a life of purpose and fulfillment. But freedom brings with it responsibility. If we are going to accept that responsibility, it means we are going to do the will of God. And that necessitates a transformation of the will. God's purpose for Israel was that it might be 'a blessing to the nations'; for that reason, he brought his people into a land of blessing. Similarly, God's purpose for us is that we might be a blessing to others. I am not sure how ''rithmatic' relates here, except to say it deals with calculation; to live a meaningful life necessitates taking a calculated view concerning life's purpose.

So then, what do we need? We need a *revelation* from God, *reconciliation* to God, and *restoration* to the purpose for which God made us. These are the objective factors which God has provided for us in Christ Jesus. They are the 'three R's' of redemption. Inwardly, we must have a transformed mind, transformed desires, and a transformed will. These are the things we need; in succeeding chapters we shall discuss how these things have been provided and how they can be ours.

Man as God made him	EFFECTS OF SIN		WHAT MAN NEEDS	
	Objective	Subjective	Objective	Subjective
Knowledge	Exchanged the truth of God	Mind set against truth	Revelation	Renewed mind
Righteousness & Holiness	Followed the way which seems right	Desires set against right	Reconcili-ation	Renewed desires
Dominion	Set at nought dominion	Will set against the will of God	Restoration	Renewed will

PART III

Man – as God Remakes Him

7: *God's Solution to the Soul's Pollution (1): The Work of Christ as Prophet*

Thomas Watson observed, 'Men in the dark cannot discern colours . . . . In the dark the greatest beauty is hid.'[1] We have already seen that sin has plunged us into intellectual and spiritual darkness, but, as a familiar epigram states, we would rather curse the darkness than light a candle. Being in darkness we cannot discern things as they really are; we need light to perceive them and to appreciate their true beauty. We need the light of truth; we need a revelation from God. The Psalmist described God's word as a lamp to his feet and a light to his path (*Ps. 119:105*). He also said, 'The unfolding of Thy words gives light; it gives understanding to the simple' (*Ps. 119:130*). When God's word penetrates the darkness of our hearts and minds, we are able to see things as they really are and to gain a true and proper perspective on life. We cannot live without the word of God. Jesus himself said, 'Man shall not live on bread alone, but on every word that proceeds out of the mouth of God' (*Matt. 4:4*). If that is really true, it is a very serious matter to ignore the light. It is equally serious to distort it, modify it, or adjust it. We may not 'hide it under a bushel' when we disagree with what it says or dislike what it reveals. We must accept what it says. Actually, that is what the Christian life is all about; we are to 'walk with the Lord in the light of his word'. Our lives are to be conformed to the will of God revealed in the scriptures. As John says, we are to 'walk in the light as He Himself is in the light' (*1 John 1:7*).

The above conclusions, of course, rest on the knowledge that the Bible is the word of God. Is such knowledge something we blindly accept without satisfactory evidence? Within the scope of

---

[1] Thomas Watson, *A Body of Divinity* (London, Banner of Truth Trust, 1958), p. 118.

biblical studies, there is one branch we call Biblical Introduction. It is an exceedingly complex field of study in which such matters as authorship, language and style, geographical data, social customs, historical incidents, and many other details are investigated in order to determine if each book of the Bible really belongs in the biblical canon. It is a scientific study to determine the context, purpose and authenticity of each book. Obviously, the content of such study is beyond the scope of our present discussion, but we can rest assured that the reliability and authenticity of all the biblical books has been well established. As the Westminster Confession of Faith says, 'it abundantly evidences itself to be the word of God'.[1] Actually, the bottom line of Biblical Introduction is to determine whether each book in the Bible bears the marks of prophetic or apostolic authorship. In other words, did the author speak on behalf of God? For example, in Jeremiah 15:19, God said to Jeremiah, 'You will become My spokesman.' The revelation of God, the light which we need, has been delivered to us by men who spoke on behalf of God. In Hebrews 1:1, we read, 'In the past God spoke to our forefathers through the prophets at many times and in various ways' (NIV). Peter said, 'men moved by the Holy Spirit spoke from God' (*2 Pet. 1:21*). God gave his revelation through prophets.

What is a prophet? The term is used rather broadly in our day. The weatherman is sometimes referred to as a prophet. With regard to sports, it is not unusual to hear commentators make their predictions about winning teams and gold medals. Then there are people, Jean Dixon for example, who claim to foretell events, and are said to possess prophetic powers. Within the church today there are many who claim to have the gift of prophecy. These usages tend to confuse us and to distort the concept of a biblical prophet. Even when we speak of a biblical prophet, there are many people who limit the term to those who foretell the future. Certainly, that is part of the prophetic ministry, but a prophet is not only one who foretells the future but also one who *forthtells* the word of God. Frequently the prophets reminded people of the law of God and called them to repentance; at other times, they explained what God was doing. Sometimes they spoke in judg-

[1] The Confession of Faith, Chapter 1, Paragraph V.

ment; at other times they brought a word of comfort. They were men who spoke on behalf of God; they proclaimed the message God had given to them. The mark of a prophet was evidenced by 'Thus saith the Lord'.

How do we know a true prophet from a false one? It is easy enough for a man to claim that he is speaking on behalf of God. There have always been those who have claimed to have visions and dreams. Indeed, the Bible is full of warnings against false prophets. How do we know which ones to believe? How do we evaluate people like Jean Dixon? From the outset, God has confirmed his word, and he has given clear guidelines by which we can determine true and false prophets:

If a prophet or a dreamer of dreams arises among you and gives you a sign or a wonder, and the sign or the wonder comes true, concerning which he spoke to you, saying, 'Let us go after other gods (whom you have not known) and let us serve them,' you shall not listen to the words of that prophet or that dreamer of dreams; for the Lord your God is testing you to find out if you love the Lord your God with all your heart and with all your soul. You shall follow the Lord your God and fear Him; and you shall keep His commandments, listen to His voice, serve Him, and cling to Him.

But that prophet or that dreamer of dreams shall be put to death, because he has counseled rebellion against the Lord your God who brought you from the land of Egypt and redeemed you from the house of slavery, to seduce you from the way in which the Lord your God commanded you to walk. So you shall purge the evil from among you (*Deut. 13:1–5*).

From this passage it is obvious that we are to be discerning; we are not to be deceived by sensational signs or wonders. Our evaluation is to be made on the basis of whether or not particular declarations are in keeping with the law of God.

In addition, in Deuteronomy 18:9–12 we are given nine different ways in which men seek to know the future:

When you enter the land which the Lord your God gives you, you shall not learn to imitate the detestable things of those nations. There shall not be found among you anyone who makes his son or his daughter pass through the fire, one who uses divination, one who practises witchcraft, or one who interprets omens, or a sorcerer, or one who casts a spell, or a medium, or a spiritist, or one who calls up the dead.

For whoever does these things is detestable to the Lord.

Within us all there is an intense desire to know the future, and sinful men will go to any lengths to discover it.

At the end of this chapter in Deuteronomy, God gives another mark of a true prophet. The test of a true prophet is that everything he says comes to pass. He is one hundred per cent accurate; God never lies or makes any mistakes. If a prophet has been sent by God, we can count on his truth and accuracy. Furthermore, God established his word at the mouth of two or three witnesses. There is agreement and also unity between what the prophets say; they bear witness to each other's integrity and trustworthiness. A true prophet, then, is one who speaks on behalf of God. He is one who brings the message of God to man. God gave his revelation to man through prophets.

The greatest prophet in the Old Testament was Moses. Through him, God revealed his law on Mount Sinai. On occasions the people murmured against him, but because he was God's representative to them, we are told that their murmuring was really against God (*Exod. 16:8*). Because Moses was the great prophet, God said to him, 'I will raise up a prophet . . . like you, and I will put My words in his mouth, and he shall speak to them all that I command him' (*Deut. 18:18*). There were, of course, numerous prophets in Israel over the centuries who followed Moses but none of them claimed to be or was recognized as being the fulfillment of this prophecy. Godly men in Israel understood this prophecy as a declaration concerning the Messiah, who, when he came, would be like Moses. After four hundred years of prophetic silence in Israel, John the Baptist appeared. His preaching attracted wide attention and caused the Jewish authorities to inquire into his identity. When they inquired if he was 'that prophet', he denied it. The Gospel tells us, however, that he was a man 'sent from God' (*John 1:6*). He was a prophetic voice sent to bear witness to Christ. Soon after the appearance of John the Baptist, Philip found Nathaniel and said to him, 'We have found Him, of whom Moses in the Law . . . wrote' (*John 1:45*). Philip is referring to Jesus as the great prophet like Moses. The purpose of the coming of Jesus was to reveal God. 'No man has seen

God at any time,' says John, 'the only begotten God . . . has explained Him' (*John 1:18*). Jesus was the great prophet predicted and anticipated by Moses. The apostles affirmed this when placed on trial before the Sanhedrin (see *Acts 3:22*). Jesus brought the full, final, and complete revelation of God; nothing can be added to what God has said in him. As Hebrews states, 'God . . . spoke long ago to the fathers in the prophets . . . in these last days [He] has spoken to us in His Son' (*Heb. 1:1–2*).

Of course, Jesus Christ is unique in that he is both the prophet and the revelation. The Shorter Catechism asks, 'What offices does Christ execute as our Redeemer?' The Answer, in part, is 'Christ as our Redeemer, executes the [office] of a prophet . . . both in his estate of humiliation and exaltation.'[1] Note the phrase, 'as our *Redeemer*'. If Christ does not execute the office of a prophet, we do not have a redeemer. Or, to say it in another way, if we are to have a redeemer, he must exercise the office of prophet and bring to us a complete revelation of God.

The Catechism proceeds to ask, 'How does Christ execute the office of a prophet?' The answer is: 'Christ executes the office of a prophet, in revealing to us, by his word and Spirit, the will of God for our salvation.'[2] Christ not only fulfilled this office when he walked the dusty roads of Palestine, that is, he not only executed it in his humiliation; he continues to fulfill this office in his exaltation. Seated at the right hand of God, he continues to exercise the office of a prophet by revealing God's will. He does so through his word and by his Spirit. In order to understand the prophetic work of Christ, we need to understand the unique nature of the word of God. We have already seen that God gave his word through holy men, but there is something more we need to understand.

When I began my theological training, I attended a very liberal college in Australia. In our first class in Bible, we were told that we should put all our prejudices and preconceived notions aside and approach the Bible like any other book. To unsuspecting students that sounded fair enough, but actually it is ridiculous. Had I known what I do now, I would have asked my teacher the question, 'Like what other book?' I have a fairly large library, and occasionally someone will ask me if I have read all my books. I

[1] The Shorter Catechism, Question 23.
[2] *Ibid.*, Question 24.

generally respond by reaching for my dictionary. I make sure the inquirer knows it is a dictionary and then I say, 'When I read this volume, I had a very difficult time understanding the drift of the story, but it certainly explained every word.' I do this not just to be funny, but to make a point. And the point is that not every book is designed or intended to be read. One cannot approach a dictionary like a missionary biography. A hymnal cannot be treated in the same way as a commentary. A book of philosophy is quite different from an encyclopedia. Some books are meant for reading, some for study, some for reference, and some for music. It is absurd to tell someone to approach the Bible like any other book.

How then are we to approach it? That which determines how we approach any book is obviously the nature of the book itself. What is the nature of the Bible? How do we approach it?

First, we need to note that it claims to be the word of God. The more we learn from archaeological discoveries and the more we study the background, the language, and the claims of the Bible, the more we are convinced that 'it abundantly evidences itself to be the word of God'. We affirm it, therefore, to be the word of God from Genesis to Revelation. It is completely without error in all of its statements, including what it says about science and history.

Though we affirm categorically that the Bible is the word of God, there is another aspect of its nature we must understand. Consider the following statements:

I waited patiently for the Lord; and He inclined to me, and heard my cry (*Ps. 40:1*).

Why are you in despair, O my soul? And why have you become disturbed within me? (*Ps. 42:5*).

I know my transgressions, and my sin is ever before me (*Ps. 51:3*).

These are just a few examples of many such statements to be found through the entire Bible. Now, the question is, are these statements the word of God? Does the Lord wait for himself? Is his soul cast down? Does he have transgressions and sin? Obviously, these are not spoken by the Lord; they are statements by men. When God gave his word, he used about forty different men. They did not all write in the same way; indeed, their personalities and abilities are evident. A competent Greek scholar, for example, could readily identify a passage written by a particular author. John, the fisherman, uses simple language whereas, Luke, the doctor, and Paul, the Pharisee, both use cultured and sophisticated words. This is where the critics stumble; the Bible is obviously the work of men; it is a thoroughly human book. The Bible cannot be treated like any other book, for it is absolutely unique; it is both the word of God *and* the word of man. It possesses two natures in one book. For that reason, it takes more than the ability to read or to parse Greek verbs to understand it.

Of course, the Lord Jesus Christ was similarly unique in that he also possessed two natures; he was truly God and truly man. It is a very serious error to try to make a distinction between the written word (the Bible) and the living Word (Jesus Christ). In the Bible they are brought together into the closest possible identity. The same terms are used to describe both, and the same attributes are applied to both. In fact, there are times when it is difficult to determine which is being considered. The point is that there is no contradiction between what God has revealed in his written revelation and what he has revealed in his Son. Jesus continues to execute the office of prophet as he speaks to us through his written word. He continues to speak through his word by his Spirit.

When Peter made his great confession of Christ at Caesarea Philippi, Jesus said, 'Blessed are you, Simon Barjonas, because flesh and blood did not reveal this to you, but My Father who is in heaven' (*Matt. 16:17*). In other words, Peter's understanding did not come because he had superior intelligence or ability; it came because God revealed it to him. In 1 Corinthians chapter 2, Paul speaks of 'Things which eye has not seen and ear has not heard, and which have not entered the heart of man, all that God has prepared for those who love him' (*v.9*). There is no way to understand the things of God simply by using the eye in observation, the ear in speculation, or the heart in appreciation. How then do we understand the things of God? The apostle goes on to tell us that 'God revealed them through the Spirit' (*v.10*). The same Spirit who inspired the prophets to write the word of God, comes to enlighten our minds to understand that same word. This does not mean that he does not use human instruments. To the contrary, he has given to his church, apostles, prophets, evangelists, pastors, and teachers (*Eph. 4:11*). What role do they play? Since the biblical canon is complete, there is no need for any additional revelation. The task of apostles and prophets is accomplished. Those who now exercise the ministry of an evangelist, pastor, or teacher (or teaching pastors), are prophets only in the sense that they proclaim the revelation that has already been given.

And what is that revelation? Christ, as our prophet, reveals to us 'the will of God for our salvation'. What is the will of God? In a general sense, all of the scripture is a declaration of God's will. It is God's will that we live by 'every word that proceeds out of the mouth of God' (*Matt. 4:4*). We are told clearly, 'This is the will of God, your sanctification' (*1 Thess. 4:3*). We are told also, 'In every thing give thanks: for this is the will of God' (*1 Thess. 5:18 KJV*). When we pray, we are to say, 'Thy will be done' (*Matt. 6:10*). In asking that, we are asking God for *active* obedience to do all he has commanded. Also, we are asking for *passive* obedience to accept whatever he sends. The whole point of Christ's prophetic office is that we might know the truth and be set free. We need the information God has given in the revelation that the *context* of our thinking might be accurate and the *content* right. He has given that revelation that we might see things as they really are, that we might have the right values and place our priorities where they should be. As Prophet-Redeemer, Christ reveals to us the will of God for our salvation. In Jesus Christ, we see what God is like. We see also what we are to be like. God says, 'This is My beloved Son, with whom I am well pleased; hear Him!' (*Matt. 17:5*). 'We must pay much closer attention', therefore, 'to what we have heard, lest we drift away from it' (*Heb. 2:1*).

Man as God made him	Man as sin made him	What man needs	What God has done	Example
Knowledge	Darkened in understanding	Revelation Renewed mind	Sent his prophets to bring the truth	Moses
Righteousness & Holiness	Unrighteous	Reconciliation Renewed desires		
Dominion	Slaves of corruption	Restoration Renewed will		

8: *God's Solution to the Soul's Pollution (2): The Work of Christ as Priest*

In his excellent book *Go Free!* Robert Horn tells what happened at a particular university when Christian students distributed a leaflet containing the first two chapters of the book of Romans, chapters which deal with 'the wrath of God and the nature and extent of human sin'. He reports that:

Student reaction was very definite. One girl came up to a bookstall and said accusingly, 'You're making us all feel guilty!' The Gay Society took sharp exception to Paul's plain speaking. Some of the Student Union committee tried to get the copies banned and the Christian Union ejected. The student newspaper published irate letters. Why were people so incensed? Why should a 1,900-year-old letter provoke them so much?

Christian Union members commented that it was not the 'Smile, Jesus loves you' approach that prompted these reactions. It was the truth about the basic relationship of God and man – the truths of wrath and sin and judgment.[1]

It is interesting indeed that a university campus where political radicals, religious fanatics, and moral perverts are permitted to voice their ideas freely should react so dramatically to a passage from the Bible. Sin and guilt are real even though we might try 'to suppress the truth' concerning them.

Because of sin, there is a great moral gulf between God and man; God is holy and we are unholy. More than that, we are 'under His wrath and curse'. God 'cannot accept us unless something is done about our sin. Sin brings guilt and guilt requires punishment.'[2]

---

[1]Robert M. Horn, *Go Free!* (London, Inter-Varsity Press, 1976), p. 8.
[2]*Ibid.*, p. 15.

71

Someone wrote the following letter to Billy Graham:

Dear Dr. Graham:

I did something very wrong some months ago – something I am ashamed to admit to anyone. I have prayed and prayed, asking God's forgiveness, but I don't feel He has forgiven me. What can I do?[1]

This person recognizes guilt and is under the burden of it. Something must be done to remove that sin and guilt before he can stand before God with a clear conscience. How are sin and guilt removed? How are we *reconciled* to God? Though the above letter does not give much information, it does reveal two basic problems. First, its writer says, 'I have prayed and prayed.' Probably, like many people today, the person thinks that sin and guilt are removed by prayer. Prayer is not the means of atonement for sin; we are not reconciled to God by prayer. We can pray loud and long but that will never remove the guilt and clear the conscience. Also, the writer says, 'I don't feel he has forgiven me.' Feelings do enter in but they are not of primary importance. There are many people who break the law of God and declare, 'I don't feel guilty.' Feelings may be quite beside the point; if God's holy law has been broken, the offender is guilty whether he feels like it or not. Because God is 'infinite, eternal, and unchangeable in his . . . justice', he does not condone or excuse sin. God does not bend the rules; he does not overlook sin. And his justice demands satisfaction equal to the offense.

Sin and guilt cannot be removed unless atonement is made. Many people, of course, try to make atonement for their sins by compensation, restitution, works of penance, humanitarian acts, or religious zeal. Actually, there are only two alternatives: either we pay the penalty ourselves or we find a satisfactory substitute. As sinners, we stand under God's wrath and curse, and as Hebrews 9:22 makes clear, 'Without shedding of blood there is no forgiveness.' Either we must die for our sins or we must find a substitutionary sacrifice. That a substitutionary sacrifice has been provided is the theme of the whole Bible. When Abraham took his son Isaac up Mount Moriah, Isaac asked, 'Behold, the fire and the wood, but where is the lamb for the burnt offering?' Abraham

---

[1] *Gazette Telegraph*, Colorado Springs, Colorado, Wed., 24 Nov. 1982.

replied, 'God will provide for Himself the lamb' (*Gen. 22:7–8*). As Abraham was about to offer Isaac, God drew his attention to a ram caught in the bushes; God provided a substitute. When Israel was about to leave Egypt, God instructed each family to take a lamb, kill it, and apply its blood to the doorposts. Either the first-born died or the lamb died; the lamb became the substitute. Similarly, the entire sacrificial system described in the Book of Leviticus is based upon the principle of substitution. If we are to go free, a satisfactory substitutionary sacrifice must be made for our sin. If we are to stand before God with a free conscience, a sacrifice must be made which will appease God's wrath and remove his curse.

What kind of substitute do we need? Obviously, it cannot be someone who is stained with sin and carries a burden of guilt himself. If that were the case, he would have to bear his own sin. The good news of the gospel is that the Lord Jesus Christ lived a perfect and sinless life; he was, therefore, able to offer himself as a substitute for you and me. Through the sacrifice of himself, he has made atonement for sin. Through his death, he has satisfied God's justice and hence appeased God's wrath and removed his curse. He alone can reconcile us to God. Charles Wesley wrote:

> Arise, my soul, arise,
> Shake off thy guilty fears:
> The bleeding Sacrifice
> In my behalf appears.[1]

Our reconciliation to God is not dependent upon our prayer or upon our feelings; it is accomplished by the sacrifice.

The sacrifice alone, however, is not all we need. Picture an Israelite, who, being conscious of his sin, finds a perfect lamb in his flock. With remorse, he takes that beautiful animal to the door of the tabernacle, confesses his sin over it, and kills it as his substitute. Is he forgiven at that point? The answer is 'No'. He must not only offer the sacrifice; that sacrifice must also be presented to God. Having offered the sacrifice, can that man enter into the holy place? Of course not! He not only needs a substitutionary sacrifice, but he must also have someone who will present his sacrifice to God. No ordinary person could enter into

---

[1] *Trinity Hymnal*, Hymn 223: 'Arise, my soul, arise'.

the tabernacle because that was a privilege reserved exclusively for the priest. The office of priest came under very strict regulation. It is most significant that the instructions regulating the office of priest are followed by the account of Nadab and Abihu, two sons of Aaron, who ignored what God said and tried to fulfill their offices in their own way (*Lev. 10*).

Hebrews 5:1 says that 'every high priest taken from among men is appointed on behalf of men in things pertaining to God in order to offer both gifts and sacrifices for sins'. He is 'taken *from among* men' and 'appointed *for* men'. In writing to Timothy, the apostle Paul says, there is 'one mediator also between God and men, the *man* Christ Jesus' (*I Tim. 2:5*; my emphasis). Why does Paul place such stress upon the humanity of Jesus Christ? He does so because Jesus Christ is our great high priest; he is our mediator. He pleads our case; he represents us before God. He has not only offered a perfect sacrifice to satisfy divine justice but he also presents the sacrifice to God on our behalf. As John Newton wrote:

> He has washed us with his blood,
> He presents our souls to God.[1]

In the previous chapter we saw that a prophet is one who comes from God to man. He represents God to men. The priest, however, goes from man to God. That is why he is taken 'from among men'. When we place these two offices together, it will be obvious why our Lord Jesus Christ has to be both God and man in order to be our Savior. As prophet, he represents God to us; as priest, he represents us to God. The Catechism asks,

Who is the Redeemer of God's elect?

The only Redeemer of God's elect is the Lord Jesus Christ, who, being the eternal Son of God, became man, and so was, and continues to be, God and man in two distinct natures, and one person, for ever.[2]

As the God-man, he is the *only* Redeemer.

'What offices does Christ execute as our Redeemer?' We saw only part of the answer in the previous chapter. 'Christ, as our Redeemer, executes the offices of a prophet, and of a priest . . .

---

[1]*Ibid.*, Hymn 127: 'Let us love, and sing, and wonder'.
[2]The Shorter Catechism, Question 21.

both in his estate of humiliation and exaltation.'[1] As I said previously, if Christ does not execute these offices, we do not have a Redeemer.

How does Christ execute the office of a priest?

Christ executes the office of a priest, in his once offering up of himself a sacrifice to satisfy divine justice, and reconcile us to God; and in making continual intercession for us.[2]

He is both the sacrifice and the priest; he *reconciles us to God*.

Let me draw your attention to the fact that Jesus Christ executes these offices 'both in his estate of humiliation and exaltation'. So far, we have been talking about his humiliation. 'He humbled Himself by becoming obedient to the point of death, even death on a cross' (*Phil. 2:8*). His sacrificial work on Calvary and his ascension to the right hand of God are part of his priestly work. How does he execute the office of a priest now? Hebrews 4:14–16 gives a beautiful answer: 'Since then we have a great high priest who has passed through the heavens, Jesus the Son of God, . . . let us therefore draw near with confidence to the throne of grace.' How do I know that when I stand before God he will not say to me, 'Depart from Me, accursed [one]' (*Matt. 25:41*)? There are many people who say that their God is a God of love who would never send anyone to hell. If my hope is based upon some such romantic notion as that, I can have no assurance that my sin is forgiven and that I am at peace with God. The reason I know that God will not turn me away is because of my great high priest who pleads my case. I am able to draw near to God because I have a high priest in the heavens. As my high priest, what is Christ doing there? He is 'making continual intercession for me'. This is the truth of Charles Wesley's hymn:

> Arise, my soul, arise!
> Shake off thy guilty fears;
> The bleeding Sacrifice
> In my behalf appears:
> Before the throne my Surety stands,
> My name is written on His hands.

[1] *Ibid.*, Question 23.
[2] *Ibid.*, Question 25.

He ever lives above,
For me to intercede;
His all-redeeming love,
His precious blood to plead;
His blood atoned for all our race,
And sprinkles now the throne of grace.

Five bleeding wounds He bears,
Received on Calvary;
They pour effectual prayers,
They strongly plead for me:
'Forgive him, O forgive,' they cry,
'Nor let that ransomed sinner die!'

The Father hears Him pray,
His dear anointed one;
He cannot turn away
The presence of His Son;
His Spirit answers to the blood,
And tells me I am born of God.

My God is reconciled;
His pard'ning voice I hear;
He owns me for His child,
I can no longer fear;
With confidence I now draw nigh,
And 'Father, Abba, Father' cry.[1]

The sacrifices in the Old Testment were a type or picture, and, therefore, they could not 'make the worshiper perfect in conscience' (*Heb. 9:9*). Similarly, prayer is good, but if my hope for reconciliation to God rests upon it, I can never be sure that I have prayed correctly. Good works are important, but if my trust is in them, I can never know if I have done enough. 'Though I give my body to be burned', I cannot atone for my sin and cast off my guilt. By contrast, says the Epistle to the Hebrews, 'How much more will the blood of Christ, who through the eternal Spirit offered Himself without blemish to God, cleanse your conscience from dead works to serve the living God?' (*9:14*). Because of the blood of Christ, we have 'confidence to enter the holy place' (*Heb. 10:19*). Therefore, 'let us draw near with a sincere heart in full

---

[1] *Songs For Worship* (Zondevan, Grand Rapids), Hymn 49:'Arise, my soul, arise!'

assurance of faith, having our hearts sprinkled clean from an evil conscience' (*Heb. 10:22*). When we know who Jesus is, what he has done, and what he is presently doing, and when we have committed our case into his hands, we are able to approach God with confidence.

Is it not significant that the author of Hebrews, having explained these things, goes on to emphasize the importance of faith? He says, 'do not throw away your confidence' (*10:35*), for we are 'of those who have faith to the preserving of the soul' (*v.39*). Faith is believing what God says, what he has said about his Son. When we believe that, we can be sure that our sins are forgiven and can have a clear conscience. We will investigate this matter further when we discuss the application of redemption. We can know, however, that 'as far as the east is from the west, so far has He removed our transgressions from us' (*Ps. 103:12*). They are buried in 'the depths of the sea' (*Mic. 7:19*). Because Christ is the great high priest who has sacrificed himself, God says, 'I will forgive their iniquity, and their sin I will remember no more' (*Jer. 31:34*). 'How blessed is he whose transgression is forgiven, whose sin is covered! How blessed is the man to whom the Lord does not impute iniquity, and in whose spirit there is no deceit!' (*Ps. 32:1–2*).

In discussing the office of Christ as prophet, we saw that Moses is the great Old Testament example. Concerning the office of priest, God says, 'I will raise up for Myself a faithful priest who will do according to what is in My heart and in My soul; and I will build him an enduring house, and he will walk before My anointed always' (*1 Sam. 2:35*). This verse, I believe, refers to Samuel, one of the greatest men in history, who pulled the nation together after four hundred years of anarchy and chaos. Samuel was a Levite and was therefore qualified to be a priest. The thing which distinguished him, however, is the fact that every time the nation experienced a crisis, Samuel was on his knees before God. His name means 'heard of God'. Every time he is mentioned outside the historical context of 1 Samuel, he is referred to as a man of intercession. It was Samuel who said, 'far be it from me that I should sin against the Lord by ceasing to pray for you' (*1 Sam. 12:23*). What a tremendous picture of our Lord Jesus; every time we go through a crisis of sin, he does not cease to pray for us. He 'ever lives to make intercession for us'.

WHAT MAN NEEDS	WHAT GOD HAS DONE		Example
	He has sent	To bring	
Revelation **Renewed mind**	Prophet	Truth	Moses (*Deut. 18:18*)
Reconciliation **Renewed desires**	Priest	Sacrifice	Samuel (*1 Sam. 2:35*)
Restoration **Renewed will**			

9: *God's Solution to the Soul's Pollution (3): The Work of Christ as King*

The first verse of the Book of Judges reads, 'the sons of Israel inquired of the Lord saying, "Who shall go up first for us against the Canaanites, to fight against them?"' That question begins a new era in the history of Israel; while Moses and Joshua were alive, there was no need to ask that question. But now Joshua was dead and the nation without a leader. The Lord's answer was that Judah should lead. Actually the Israelites should have known that. Genesis 49:10 reveals that Judah would be the tribe through which the king would come and, all along, Judah had led the marches. During the following four hundred years (the period covered in the Book of Judges), the nation became fragmented and chaotic. The reason, we are told, was, 'in those days there was no king in Israel; every man did what was right in his own eyes' (*Judg. 17:6; 18:1; 19:1; 21:25*). There are some who teach that it was wrong for Israel to have a king, that God intended that he should be their king. But the Book of Judges shows clearly what happens when there is no human king; it shows us too how God made the Israelites acutely aware of their need for such a king. The Book of Ruth is actually an appendix to Judges; its importance lies in the fact that it introduces God's chosen king, David (*Ruth 4:22*).

One of the first things David did as king was to go up to Jerusalem and conquer it. For the four hundred years Israel had been in the land, Jerusalem had been in the hands of the Jebusites. In other words, the chief citadel of the nation was in enemy hands. When the Jebusites saw David and his men coming, they said, '"You shall not come in here, but the blind and lame shall turn you away"; thinking, "David cannot enter here." Nevertheless, David captured the stronghold of Zion, that is the city of David' (*2 Sam. 5:6–7*). Having captured the chief citadel, David went on to expand the borders to the full extent of the boundaries that God had promised Abraham (see *Josh. 21:43-45, 2 Sam. 8:3, 1 Kings 8:65, 2 Chron. 7:8*). 'The Lord helped David wherever he went' (*2 Sam. 8:6, 14*). He conquered the enemies on every side and established peace.

'What offices does Christ execute as our Redeemer?' 'Christ, as our Redeemer, executes the offices of a prophet, of a priest, and *of a king*, both in his estate of humiliation and exaltation'[1] (my emphasis). As Moses was the great example of Christ's prophetic office and Samuel of his priestly office, David is the example of his kingly office. More than that, it was promised that the Messiah would come from the family of David. In 2 Samuel 7:16, we read God's promise to David:

Your house and your kingdom shall endure before Me forever; your throne shall be established forever.

That Christ was to come from the tribe of Judah and from the family of David is evident in many Old Testament prophecies. God promised Jacob, that 'the scepter shall not depart from Judah' (*Gen. 49:10*). Then, down through the centuries, the prophets constantly reminded Israel that Messiah would come from the house of David. For example:

His name will be called Wonderful Counselor, Mighty God, Eternal Father, *Prince* of Peace. There will be no end to the increase of His *government* or of peace, on *the throne of David*, and over *his kingdom*, to establish it and to uphold it with justice and righteousness from then on and forevermore (*Isa. 9:6-7*; my emphasis).

You, Bethlehem Ephrathah [the city of David], . . . from you One will go forth for Me to be *ruler* in Israel (*Mic. 5:2*; my emphasis).

The kingship of Christ is a prominent Old Testament theme. David himself devoted three entire Psalms to this theme and, of course, made many passing references to it (see *Ps. 45; 72; 110*). He declared that God has set his king upon the holy hill of Zion (*Ps. 2:6*). In writing about the triumphal entry, Zechariah declared:

[1] The Shorter Catechism, Question 26.

Rejoice greatly, O daughter of Zion! Shout in triumph, O daughter of Jerusalem! Behold, *your king* is coming to you; He is just and endowed with salvation (*Zech. 9:9*; my emphasis).

In speaking of the second coming of Christ, Daniel wrote:

One like the Son of man came with the clouds of heaven . . . and there was given him *dominion*, and glory, and a *kingdom*, that all people, nations, and languages, should serve him: his *dominion* is an everlasting *dominion*, which shall not pass away, and his *kingdom* that which shall not be destroyed (*Dan. 7:13–14 KJV*; my emphasis).

One thousand years after David, the angel Gabriel visited a lowly maid and announced to her that she had been chosen by God to be the mother of the Messiah. He said:

You will . . . bear a son, and you shall name Him Jesus. He will be great, and will be called the Son of the Most High; and the Lord God will give Him *the throne of His father David*; and He will *reign* over the house of Jacob forever; and *His kingdom* will have no end (*Luke 1:31–33*; my emphasis).

When Jesus was born, Matthew tells us that wise men from the East came seeking him who had been born 'King of the Jews' (*Matt. 2:1–2*). When Jesus began his ministry, he went every-where 'proclaiming the gospel *of the kingdom*' (*Matt. 4:23*; my emphasis). On one occasion, a blind beggar sat by the roadside; he had heard that Jesus was coming. As Jesus drew near, Bartimaeus cried out: 'Jesus, *Son of David*, have mercy on me!' (*Mark 10:47*; my emphasis). In using the title, 'Son of David', he acknowledged that Jesus was the Messiah. Apparently he knew that when the Messiah comes, 'the eyes of the blind will be opened, and the ears of the deaf will be unstopped' (*Isa. 35:5*). Jesus did not come as an earthly king with a great display of pomp and glory; he demon-strated his kingship by opening the eyes of a poor blind beggar. This king cared for his subjects. Matthew begins his Gospel with wise men seeking 'the King of the Jews' and ends it with mocking men nailing an accusation to the cross of Jesus: 'THIS IS JESUS THE KING OF THE JEWS' (*Matt. 27:37*). In his birth, ministry, death, resurrection, ascension, and coming again, Jesus Christ is King of kings and Lord of lords. It is not surprising that the opening phrase of the New Testament is: 'The book of the genealogy of Jesus Christ, the *son of David*' (*Matt. 1:1*; my emphasis).

But what does the kingship of Christ mean to us? How does it relate to and affect our salvation? As we have seen, we were made to have 'dominion'. Instead of fulfilling the purpose and exercising the role for which we were made, we have gone our own way and 'done our own thing'. Consequently, we are under the dominion of sin; we are slaves of corruption. We need to be brought out of our spiritual bondage and restored to the place where we fulfill the purpose for which God made us. Salvation involves liberation, not only from the penalty of sin but also from its power. In order to liberate us and restore us, our Lord Jesus Christ executes the office of a King. 'How does Christ execute the office of a king?' 'Christ executes the office of a king, in subduing us to himself, in ruling and defending us, and in restraining and conquering all his and our enemies.'[1]

I mentioned earlier that the first thing David did when he became king was to conquer Jerusalem, at the heart of the nation. The first thing the Lord Jesus Christ does as our King is to 'subdue us to himself'. As sinners, our hearts are in the hands of the enemy. We are rebels with wills set against the rule and reign of God. Obviously, that willful opposition to and rebellion against God must be broken. He will break down that stubborn opposition through grace or through his rule with 'a rod of iron'. When we consider the application of redemption, we will discuss how he subdues us to himself. At this point, we must understand that if we have not been subdued to Christ, we cannot claim him as our Redeemer. One of the subtle errors that has permeated the church in recent times is the notion that a person can claim Jesus Christ as Savior without owning him as Lord. If we do not own him as King, we cannot claim to be his subjects. If we are in his kingdom, he is our King. The eminent theologian, Charles Hodge, writes:

Every believer recognizes Christ as his absolute Sovereign; Lord of his inward, as well as of his outward, life. He yields to Him the entire subjection of the reason, of the conscience, and of the heart. He makes

---

[1]*Ibid.*, Question 26.

Him the object of reverence, love, and obedience. In Him he trusts for protection from all enemies, seen and unseen. On Him he relies for help in every emergency, and for final triumph.[1]

If we have been translated out of the kingdom of darkness into the kingdom of light, our desires will be to 'hallow His name, further His kingdom, and do His will'. When Christ subdues us to himself, our desire will be to please him and to do his will. The subjects of his kingdom are characterized by love and obedience.

Our Lord not only 'subdues us to himself', he 'rules and defends us'. His word becomes the rule for our faith and practice. We willingly obey what he commands. Again, Charles Hodge says,

The laws of the kingdom . . . require . . . that His people should be holy in heart and life. They must be poor in spirit; meek; merciful; peace-makers; long suffering; ready to forgive; . . . not seeking their own; bearing all things; believing all things; and hoping all things. They are forbidden to be avaricious [greedy for riches], or covetous, or proud, or worldly minded. In one word, they are required to be like Christ, in disposition, character, and conduct.[2]

King Jesus rules his people with justice and equity. The yoke he places on his subjects is easy and his burden is light (*Matt. 11:30*). Indeed, the apostle Paul delighted to refer to himself as a 'bond-slave of Jesus Christ'. Jesus Christ not only rules his people but also defends them. When he sends his servants out to difficult and dangerous missions, he says, 'Lo, I am with you always, even to the end of the age' (*Matt. 28:20*). He is a king who knows each subject personally and watches over each one individually.

Having conquered Jerusalem, David expanded the borders of the land. We often tend to place this aspect first in Christian experience. We try to expand the borders of our Christian lives when the heart has not been subdued and remains in the hand of the enemy. In our prayer, we sometimes pray, 'Thy kingdom come.' That is a profound request; it involves many aspects. In it, we are requesting by implication that the kingdom of Satan be terminated and destroyed. We are asking that the kingdom of darkness be overturned by the kingdom of light. We are

---

[1]Charles Hodge, *Systematic Theology*, Vol. II (London, James Clarke, 1960), p. 601.
[2]*Ibid.*, p. 603.

expressing the desire that the glorious kingdom of our Lord be consummated.

There are two major aspects to the kingdom of our Lord Jesus Christ. First, it is a kingdom of grace. On one occasion, the Lord was asked by the Pharisees when the kingdom of God would come. He replied, 'The kingdom of God is not coming with signs to be observed; nor will they say, "Look, here it is!" or, "There it is!" For behold, the kingdom of God is in your midst' (*Luke 17:20–21*). Though I am redeemed by grace, I look within and what do I find? I find within myself a heart that is deceitful above all things. I find a heart that contains covetousness, pride, greed, selfishness and all manner of things which displease my King. As Paul said, 'I joyfully concur with the law of God in the inner man, but I see a different law in the members of my body waging war against the law of my mind, and making me a prisoner of the law of sin which is in my members. Wretched man that I am! Who will set me free . . .?' (*Rom. 7:22–24*). When I pray, 'Thy kingdom come,' I am asking King Jesus to expand the borders of grace within my soul. I am asking him to make me more obedient and willing. I am asking him to 'restrain and conquer' the opposition within my soul. 'He breaks the pow'r of reigning sin, He sets the pris'ner free.'[1]

This petition contains the request that the borders of the kingdom of grace will be enlarged in the lives of others also. It involves the desire that others will be brought into the kingdom of grace; in this petition there is a strong missionary concept. That means that when we use this petition, we are asking that the world, the devil, and the flesh will be 'restrained and conquered'. These are our enemies and King Jesus alone is able to overcome them.

The kingdom of our Lord is also a kingdom of glory. When we pray, 'Thy kingdom come,' we are expressing the desire that the kingdom of Christ will be finally consummated and the kingdom of Satan and darkness finally destroyed. We are anticipating that time when 'the kingdom of this world has become the kingdom of our Lord, and of His Christ' (*Rev. 11:15*). We are asking that the day might be hastened when the King himself 'will descend from heaven with a shout' and the saints 'be caught up . . . to meet the Lord in the air' (*1 Thess. 4:16–17*). This petition anticipates the

---

[1] *Trinity Hymnal*, Hymn 133: 'O for a thousand tongues to sing'.

time when 'the earth will be filled with the knowledge of the glory of the Lord, as the waters cover the sea' (*Hab. 2:14*). That will happen only when King Jesus has finally 'conquered all his enemies and ours'.

Satan took Jesus to a high mountain and showed him all the kingdoms of the world. He said, 'All these [kingdoms] will I give You, if You fall down and worship me' (*Matt. 4:9*). That would have been an easy course; Jesus could have avoided the cross. At least, that was the temptation. But Jesus did not come to obtain kingdoms; while there are kingdoms, kingdom will rise against kingdom (*Matt. 24:7*). Jesus came to purchase a kingdom. To do so, he 'disarmed the rulers and authorities; he made a public display of them, having triumphed over them' (*Col. 2:15*). He came to purchase a kingdom in which the subjects are both willing and obedient. Did not the Old Testament prophets say that God would 'give [his people] a new heart and put a new spirit' in them and cause them to walk in his statutes and obey his command-ments (*Ezek. 36:26–27*)? King Jesus 'restrains and conquers all his and our enemies'.

How wonderful to know that 'sin shall not have dominion over you' because 'death hath no more dominion over him' (*Rom. 6:14, 9 KJV*). As our King, Jesus subdues us to himself; he rules and defends us, and he restrains and conquers all his enemies and ours. We are set free. Like Moses empowered by God in Egypt, Christ has come, conquered the 'Egyptians', and brought us out of the mud pits of sin. He has done so, however, for a reason. He has not set us free to wander all our lives in a wilderness. He has set us free that we might fulfill the purpose for which God made us. If he truly is our King, we are his subjects. And as his subjects, we are under his orders. He has said, 'All authority has been given to Me . . . go therefore' (*Matt. 28:18–19*). He has committed to us the responsi-bility of spreading the news about his kingdom. We are to glorify him 'by loving him and doing what he commands'.[1] Only when we are obedient to his will do we find meaning, fulfillment, satisfac-tion, and purpose in life.

The amazing thing about being in Christ's kingdom is that, though we are his subjects, he makes us kings. He 'hath made us

[1]*Catechism For Young Children* (Great Commission Publications, Philadelphia, n.d.), Question 4.

kings and priests unto God' (*Rev. 1:6 KJV*). He has 'made us unto our God kings and priests: and we shall reign on the earth' (*Rev. 5:10 KJV*). Equally wonderful is the statement in Romans 5:17: 'those who receive the abundance of grace and of the gift of righteousness will *reign in life* through the One, Jesus Christ' (my emphasis). If you want to reign in life, you must receive the abundance of grace and the gift of righteousness.

As our *prophet*, Christ has brought to us the full, final, and complete *revelation*; he has done so to meet our intellectual need. As our *priest*, he has offered a complete and perfect sacrifice to *reconcile* us to God; he has done so to meet our moral need. As our *king*, he subdues us to himself and restrains and conquers our enemies; he does so to *restore* us to the purpose for which we were made. As prophet, priest, and king, the work of Christ exactly fits our need. Perhaps this will help us to appreciate our Lord's words when he said, 'I am the way [priest], and the truth [prophet], and the life [king]; no one comes to the Father, but through Me' (*John 14:6*). You will remember, however, that we need not only revelation, reconciliation, and restoration; we need a renewed mind, renewed desires, and a renewed will. We will turn our attention in the next study to see how the redemption purchased by Christ is applied to our lives.

Isaac Watts sums up the offices of Christ in his great hymn:

> Join all the glorious names
> Of wisdom, love, and power,
> That mortals ever knew,
> That angels ever bore;
> All are too mean to speak His worth,
> Too mean to set my Savior forth.

> Great *Prophet* of my God,
> My tongue would bless Thy name:
> By Thee the joyful news
> Of our salvation came,
> The joyful news of sins forgiv'n
> Of hell subdued and peace with heav'n.

> Jesus, my great *High Priest*,
> Offered His blood, and died;
> My guilty conscience seeks
> No sacrifice beside:

His pow'rful blood did once atone
And now it pleads before the throne.

My Savior and my Lord,
My Conquer'r and *my King*,
Thy sceptre and Thy sword,
Thy reigning grace I sing:
Thine is the pow'r: behold I sit
In willing bonds beneath Thy feet.[1]

WHAT MAN NEEDS	WHAT GOD HAS DONE		Example	Jesus is
	He sent a	To bring		
Revelation **Renewed Mind**	Prophet	Truth	Moses	Truth
Reconciliation **Renewed Desires**	Priest	Sacrifice	Samuel	Way
Restoration **Renewed Will**	King	Freedom	David	Life

[1]*Hymns* (Chicago, Inter-Varsity Christian Fellowship, 1954), Hymn 48: 'Join all the glorious names'.

10: *The Application of Redemption (1): The Holy Spirit Enlightens the Mind*

Two basic things are necessary for us to see: we need both light and sight. Though our vision might be perfect, we cannot see when we are in total darkness. And, on the other hand, though we stand in the full blaze of the noon-day sun, we will not see if we have no sight. The same is true spiritually. God has sent his Prophet to bring us the revelation that is our spiritual light. The Psalmist says, 'Thy word is a lamp to my feet, and a light to my path' (*Ps. 119:105*). The apostle John says, 'the true Light which, coming into the world, enlightens every man' (*John 1:9*). The revelation provides us with all the light (or information) we need. There is nothing wrong with the light; the problem is with our sight.

The city of Dothan had been surrounded by the army of Syria, and Elisha's servant, seeing the vast military force, cried, 'Alas, my master! What shall we do?' (*2 Kings 6:15*). Elisha answered, 'Do not fear, for those who are with us are more than those who are with them' (*v.16*). Elisha saw the total picture; his servant, however, couldn't see beyond his physical situation. Elisha prayed for his servant and said, '"O Lord . . . open his eyes, that he may see." And the Lord opened the servant's eyes, and he saw; and behold, the mountain was full of horses and chariots of fire all around Elisha' (*v.17*). To see things in their proper perspective, he needed to have his eyes opened. Though we have the light of God's word, we still fail to see because we are spiritually blind. We need, as Paul says, to have the eyes of our heart enlightened (*Eph. 1:18*). The Psalmist recognized his need and prayed, 'Open my eyes, that I may behold wonderful things from Thy law' (*Ps. 119:18*). In other words, God has provided the *objective* factor in giving us light but we still need a *subjective* work within us.

Previously, we have seen the problem of our sinfulness, and we have seen the solution to that problem in Jesus Christ. Now, we need to understand how that solution can be applied to the problem. The Catechism asks, 'How are we made partakers of the redemption purchased by Christ?' 'We are made partakers of the redemption purchased by Christ, by the effectual application of it to us by his Holy Spirit.'[1] There are many people who regard the work of the Holy Spirit as mysterious, mystical and completely inexplicable. On the contrary, his work is practical and fits our need precisely. In this study, I want to consider how the Holy Spirit works in our minds to bring us to understand the truth.

In our discussion of revelation, we saw that the written word (the Bible) and the living Word (Jesus Christ) are both human and divine; both have two natures in one body. It is helpful to understand the role of the Holy Spirit in this relationship. First, the Holy Spirit was active in the incarnation of Jesus: when the angel Gabriel appeared to Mary and announced to her that she would be the mother of the Messiah, he said, 'The Holy Spirit will come upon you' (*Luke 1:35*). The work of the Holy Spirit in the life of Christ did not end there. When Jesus was baptized, the Holy Spirit descended upon him (*Luke 3:22*). Throughout his ministry, Jesus was 'full of the Holy Spirit' (*Luke 4:1*), and went about 'in the power of the Spirit' (*Luke 4:14*). Obviously, the Holy Spirit not only initiated the incarnation but also continued to be active in the life and ministry of Jesus, the living Word. Thus we are not surprised that Jesus told his disciples that when the Spirit came (at Pentecost), he would '*bear witness* of Me' (*John 15:26*; my emphasis) and '*glorify* Me' (*John 16:14*). The Holy Spirit did not come in competition to Jesus but in order that Jesus might be known and glorified.

Similarly, the Holy Spirit was active in the inspiration of the written word. 'Men moved by the Holy Spirit spoke from God' (*2 Pet. 1:21*). He initiated the word of God, but his work does not end there: he continues to work through it. And, just as he does not compete with Jesus, he does not compete with the word he has already given. What the Holy Spirit says is always in keeping with his word; it is never contrary to it.

[1] The Shorter Catechism, Question 29.

Again, it should be stressed that there is nothing wrong with that word; it provides the proper *context* and the right *content* for our thinking. The problem is with our spiritual sight, our lack of understanding. In quoting Isaiah, the apostle Paul says that spiritual things are those 'things which eye has not seen and ear has not heard, and which have not entered the heart of man' (*1 Cor. 2:9*). Thus, according to the testimony of both the Old and New Testaments, we cannot get spiritual things into our hearts and minds by physical effort, intellectual ability, or special insight. How then do we perceive the things of God? The passage goes on to say, 'God revealed them through the Spirit; for the Spirit searches all things, even the depths of God' (*1 Cor. 2:10*). In using the word 'reveal', Paul is not saying that the Holy Spirit is another prophet. We have already seen that Jesus Christ is the full, final, and complete revelation from God. We do not need any additional revelation. To claim additional revelation, as many do, is really a terrible thing: it is a declaration that Jesus Christ is not sufficient and that he has not fully revealed God. It implies, too, that the Holy Spirit failed to do what the New Testament claims he did. The Holy Spirit does not now come with a new revelation; he comes to unveil or disclose the truth we already have. He has come to open our minds to the truth of God. Jesus said, 'He will guide you into all the truth' (*John 16:13*). In praying for the Ephesians, Paul prayed, 'that the God of our Lord Jesus Christ, the Father of glory, may give to you a spirit of wisdom and of revelation in the knowledge of Him. I pray that the eyes of your heart may be enlightened, so that you may know . . .' (*Eph. 1:17–18*). Matthew Henry believes that 'the spirit of wisdom and revelation' refers directly to the Holy Spirit. It certainly is an accurate designation. He is the one who opens the eyes of our understanding and causes us to see. The truth which the Spirit teaches us, the truth to which he opens our understanding, is the truth contained in the word he has already given.

To open our understanding, the Spirit works through his word in our minds. We do not get a renewed mind through some mysterious form of spiritual osmosis. God does not speak to an inactive or lazy mind. Our understanding will never be opened and our minds will never be transformed if we refuse to think. When Paul goes on to say that 'a natural man does not accept the things of the Spirit of God; for they are foolishness to him' (*1 Cor. 2:14*), he is not saying that the word of God is irrational, absurd, or unintelligible. God's word is given in intelligible and reasonable propositions. It is possible for a person to think about them, discuss them, and even expound them. It is, however, possible for a blind man to become a physicist and to be able to discuss the properties of light he has never seen. It is possible for a man to be spiritually blind and yet be able to talk about the light of God's word. He might know about the light, but never see. On the other hand, he will never see unless he does know about the light. 'Faith comes from hearing, and hearing by the word of Christ' (*Rom. 10:17*). The mind must be applied to the truth; the Spirit of God does not work in a vacuum.

We can go a step further. A person might have his eyes opened to the truth and yet never be converted. This appears to be assumed in the statements in Hebrews 6: 'in the case of those who have once been *enlightened* . . . and have been made partakers of the Holy Spirit, and have tasted the good word of God . . . and then have fallen away, it is impossible to renew them again to repentance' (*vv.4–5*; my emphasis). It seems as though we have here a person whose eyes have been opened to the truth; he acknowledges the word of God as the truth and then rejects it. In other words, if a person sins against the light which God the Holy Spirit gives him, nothing more can be done. In interpreting the parable of the sower and the seed, Jesus spoke of some seed being choked by thorns. He said that 'this is the man who hears the word, and the worry of the world, and the deceitfulness of riches choke the word, and it becomes unfruitful' (*Matt. 13:22*).

On one occasion, a man sat in my office and gave a clear testimony of faith in Jesus Christ; there was no doubt that he *knew* the truth. In our discussion, I learned that he was living a wicked, adulterous life. I have no question that the Spirit of God had opened that man's eyes to the truth, but that is as far as he would go. I doubt if he had ever been converted; at least, there was no basis for his claim to belong to Christ.

In the Book of Acts, we are told about three men who heard the gospel from the lips of the apostle Paul. Their responses are worthy of note:

1. Festus spoke boldly of the wisdom of the natural man; to him

the gospel was sheer nonsense. He said to Paul, 'Paul, you are out of your mind! Your great learning is driving you mad' (*Acts 26:24*).

2. Agrippa, on the other hand, was impressed and deeply moved. He responded by saying, 'Almost thou persuadest me to be a Christian' (*Acts 26:28 KJV*).

3. Felix was even more deeply moved. As Paul 'was discussing righteousness, self-control and the judgment to come, Felix became frightened' (*Acts 24:25*).

All three heard the word of God, but how different their responses! Yet, none of them, so far as we know, became Christians. The gospel proves to be either the smell of death or the fragrance of life (*2 Cor. 2:16 NIV*). If truth is not the means of conversion, it becomes the grounds for condemnation.

'How does the Spirit apply to us the redemption purchased by Christ?' 'The Spirit applies to us the redemption purchased by Christ, by working faith in us . . . .'.[1] He works faith in us as we hear the word of God. We obviously cannot believe something we do not know. 'How shall they believe in Him whom they have not heard?' (*Rom. 10:14*). The Spirit of God continues to work through the word of God. As Satan began his temptation of Adam at the tree of knowledge, the Holy Spirit begins his regenerative work in our minds; he confronts us with the truth.

The Catechism goes on to ask, 'What is effectual calling?' The part of the answer which concerns us in this study is: 'Effectual calling is the work of God's Spirit, whereby . . . *enlightening our minds* in the knowledge of Christ . . . he persuades and enables us to embrace Jesus Christ, freely offered to us in the gospel' (my emphasis).[2] The first step in conversion is: the mind must be enlightened in the knowledge of Christ. How does the Holy Spirit enlighten our minds? Some biblical examples will help answer this question.

Three people went to the tomb of our Lord on the resurrection morning. It is instructive to note what each one saw:

1. Mary came while it was still dark, and she saw that the stone had been rolled away. She saw important evidence but she completely misinterpreted it. She said, 'they have taken away

[1]*Ibid.*, Question 30.
[2]*Ibid.*, Question 31.

92

my Lord, and I do not know where they have laid Him' (*John 20:13*). There was nothing wrong with the evidence; the information she had was accurate. Her problem was not the light but her sight. The word 'saw' here is the word for *observation*.

2. Peter came to the tomb, and he saw the linen clothes lying. Peter went into the tomb and examined the grave clothes. Their appearance puzzled him. The word here is not that for observation but for *examination*. We use it when we are considering some proposition; we say 'Let me see!' Again, there was nothing wrong with the information; Peter's problem was his sight.

3. Finally, John entered the tomb and 'he saw'. The word here is a third word; it is the word for *illumination*. Occasionally, we express ourselves by saying, 'Oh, I see!' John entered the tomb and he understood; the truth of what had happened had dawned on him.

To get a true perspective on the resurrection of Jesus, both Mary and Peter had to have an interview with the risen Lord. John, on the other hand, was able to bear witness to the things he had seen and heard. John's understanding was not due to superior intelligence or more perception; it was due to the fact that the Spirit of God opened his eyes to the truth.

When the Holy Spirit opens our eyes to the truth, it is not a once-for-all experience. At Caesarea Philippi, Jesus asked his disciples, 'Who do people say that the Son of Man is?' (*Matt. 16:13*). Peter responded, 'Thou art the Christ, the Son of the living God.' 'Jesus answered, and said to him, "Blessed are you, Simon Barjonas, because flesh and blood did not reveal this to you, but My Father who is in heaven"' (*Matt. 16:17*). The identity of Jesus was not something Peter learned by 'flesh and blood'. That is, he did not come to that conclusion by logical deduction or wise speculation. He understood because God opened his eyes. Immediately afterwards, however, the Lord began to 'show His disciples that He must go to Jerusalem, and suffer many things from the elders and chief priests and scribes, and be killed, and be raised up on the third day' (*Matt. 16:21*). Hearing Jesus speak of his death, Peter began to rebuke the Lord and said, 'This shall never happen to You' (*v.22*). Jesus responded, 'Get behind Me, Satan! You are a stumbling-block to Me; for you are not setting your mind on God's interests, but man's' (*v.23*). At one moment Peter was open to the truth about Jesus; at the next moment, he was closed to instruction from the lips of the Lord he had confessed. It is obvious he did not really hear the part about the Lord being raised up on the third day; had he done so, he would not have had the problem at the tomb. The point is that we need the illumination of the Holy Spirit continually. Whenever we open the word of God, we need to pray the prayer of the Psalmist, 'Open my eyes, that I may behold wonderful things from Thy law' (*Ps. 119:18*). Unless the Spirit of God opens our eyes to the truth of the things of God, we shall remain blind.

This ministry of the Spirit is essential if we are to be saved. If the Holy Spirit does not open our spiritual eyes and thereby enable us to see the truth, we are lost. But, having come to faith in the word of God, the understanding of it, as I have already said, is not a once-for-all experience. I have been a Christian for many years; it has been my privilege to study the Bible in some of the finest schools in the world and under some of the godliest men in this generation. One would think that I should know it all, but I have discovered that the more I learn, the more I need to learn. And the more I learn, the more I realize my need for the enlightening ministry of the Holy Spirit. I shudder when I read Matthew 11:25 where Jesus says, 'Thou didst hide these things from the wise and intelligent and didst reveal them to babes.' It is so easy to come to the word of God as a 'wise and intelligent' person – after all, I have studied Greek and Hebrew! I have read many books, and the big temptation is to think that I can understand it all without the ministry of the Spirit of God. The truth is:

> The Spirit breathes upon the Word,
> And brings the truth to sight.[1]

So then, we need the word of God to give us the *information*, and we need the Spirit of God to give us the *illumination*. Both are indispensable if we are to come to faith in God. 'Without faith it is impossible to please Him' (*Heb. 11:6*). We must, on the one hand, 'pay much closer attention to what we have heard' (*Heb. 2:1*), i.e.

---

[1] *Trinity Hymnal*, Hymn 258: 'The Spirit breathes upon the Word'.

the information. And we must, on the other hand, ask the Spirit of God to open our eyes to the truth and thereby teach us, i.e the illumination. We must pray with the hymn writer,

> More about Jesus let me learn,
> More of his holy will discern;
> Spirit of God, my teacher be,
> Showing the things of Christ to me.[1]

Only as the Spirit of God teaches us will we have *believing* minds, that is, minds which operate within the right framework, and *pure* minds, that is, minds which think those things which are lovely, pure, and of good report (*Phil. 4:8*). A transformed mind is essential for salvation.

WHAT WE NEED		Work of the Spirit	To bring
Objective	Subjective		
Revelation	Renewed mind	Enlightens the mind	Faith
Reconciliation	Renewed desires		
Restoration	Renewed will		

[1] *Ibid.*, Hymn 676: 'More about Jesus would I know'.

11: *The Application of Redemption (2): The Holy Spirit Convicts the Conscience*

In applying redemption to us, the Holy Spirit begins by enlightening the eyes of our understanding; he opens our minds to grasp the truth of God's word. Knowledge of the truth, however, can be a dangerous thing: it increases personal responsibility. To know the truth yet not embrace it brings greater condemnation. There is, therefore, more to our redemption than knowledge and understanding, although these are basic. To be saved, we must have an understanding of the truth; the mind must be renewed, although such renewal is only the beginning.

The second aspect of our redemption wrought by the Holy Spirit is the conviction of the conscience to bring us to repentance. It is at this point that the Holy Spirit begins to renew our desires. Occasionally, we hear people say, 'Let conscience be your guide.' Let us consider this matter of conscience. As moral beings, we know that there is right and wrong. The conscience is that God-given faculty which exercises the roles of law and judge. We are able to do some things with a 'clear conscience' because we know they are within the limits of what is right. On the other hand, when we do something wrong or questionable, our conscience operates, and we begin to formulate excuses in case we should be discovered. When Moses slew the Egyptian, we are told 'he looked this way and that' (*Exod. 2:12*), to see if anyone was watching. The conscience acts as the law; it tells us how far we may go. When we do something which we know to be wrong, the conscience acts as judge; it condemns us and causes us to stay awake at night. D. L. Moody once said that conscience is like an alarm clock; it will arouse you at first but it is easy to fall asleep again.

It is possible to silence conscience and as the scripture says, to sear the conscience with a hot iron (*1 Tim. 4:2*), that is, to ignore the conscience to the point where one can do wrong without giving it a second thought. In fact, the longer a person remains in sin, the more insensitive his conscience becomes. And as conscience becomes weaker, sin becomes stronger. It is possible to proceed in unrighteousness until one is given over to both a reprobate mind and reprobate desires. So then, under some circumstances it might be good advice to say, 'Let conscience be your guide,' but such advice assumes too much to be a general rule. Conscience by itself is quite inadequate.

Many people live at peace with their conscience because they accept the dictates of society as to what is right and wrong. The conscience is silenced by appealing to society and claiming that 'everybody is doing it'. Our society condemns arrogance toward one's fellow men but approves blasphemy towards God, and we adjust to accept that without any pangs of conscience. Even professing Christians can silence conscience; our society tells us how to spend the Lord's Day and we accept such standards without a second thought. The conscience by itself is not adequate; to be useful, the conscience must be informed. And the information must not come from the standards set by society but from the only infallible guide for faith and practice. When we know what our God requires of us, then we have the right framework for the conscience.

The apostle Paul serves as an excellent example. In Romans 7:7 he says he had not known sin. Although he was a most religious man, he was completely unaware of sin in his life. He describes his spiritual condition as one who was a blasphemer, and a persecutor, and a violent man. He acted, he says, in ignorance and unbelief (*1 Tim. 1:13*). He could persecute Christians and even assist in the stoning of Stephen without any pangs of conscience. In fact, he considered that his conscience was blameless (*Acts 24:16*). How then did he come to be convicted of his sin? What brought him to the place where he admitted he was the foremost of sinners (*1 Tim. 1:15*)? His argument in Romans chapter 7 is clear: 'I would not have come to know sin except through the Law; for I would not have known about coveting if the Law had not said, "You shall not covet"' (*v.7*). His mind, which had been darkened by sin and blinded by religion, was suddenly confronted by the law of God, and his conscience began to act in the right framework. A sinner ignorant of God's law does not see the immensity of sin; he does not have any pangs of conscience about his conduct or the desires of his heart. Until we are confronted by the righteous demands of God's law, we cherish our unrighteous and unholy desires, and we see no need for change. The mind must know the law of God before the conscience can be aroused to see our real need.

The Holy Spirit does not enlighten our minds in a vacuum; he does so through the word of God. Similarly, it is by the law that we come to a knowledge of sin (*Rom. 3:20*). Through the word of God we are confronted with our sin; there we discover that the cherished desires of the heart are corrupt before God. It is in the word of God that we learn that not only is the outward act of adultery sin, but also the lust of the heart. It is not murder alone that is condemned, but also the attitude of hatred. When we look into God's word, we soon discover that which 'searches our hearts'. When those cherished desires come under the searchlight of truth, the Spirit of God brings conviction to the conscience.

The Spirit of God is thorough in his work of convicting the conscience; he touches our sin at many points. James Buchanan says that the Spirit of God convicts of the fact of sin, the fault of sin, the folly of sin, the filth of sin, the fountain of sin, and the fruit of sin:[1]

The Spirit of God convicts of the *fact* of sin – he shows where the law of God has been broken.

The Spirit of God convicts of the *fault* of sin – he shows the effect of the transgression on the offender and on others.

The Spirit of God convicts of the *folly* of sin – he shows how our sin is against our reason and welfare. It is utterly foolish.

The Spirit of God convicts of the *filth* of sin – he shows that it is morally corrupt.

The Spirit of God convicts of the *fountain* of sin – he shows that sin proceeds from a corrupt nature with unholy desires.

[1] James Buchanan, *The Office and Work of the Holy Spirit* (London, Banner of Truth Trust, 1966), p. 67.

The Spirit of God convicts of the *fruit* of sin – he shows that its wages are death.

One reason why we do not see much conviction of sin accompanied by tears of repentance these days is due to the fact that we neglect, or ignore, or rationalize the law of God. When we by-pass God's truth, there is no basis for genuine conviction. We do not come to conviction of sin by looking at sin; conviction comes through the law of God. The Spirit of God uses the law of God to touch the conscience.

There are many ways in which a person might respond to the convicting work of God's Spirit. Two may be mentioned here. First, there are those who enter the plea, 'not guilty'. They try to justify themselves by rationalizing their behavior and attitudes and projecting the blame on to someone else. When confronted with the word of God, they ask 'Has God said?' Or, they respond by saying, 'Surely, it doesn't mean that!' Or, they say, 'That was for Bible times; things have changed and one must keep up with the times.' What happens is that the word of God is placed on trial; if its authority can be avoided or minimized, the conscience can go free. Of course, any attempt to justify ourselves in the light of God's word only increases our guilt. And while we might silence an uneasy conscience, we grieve the Spirit of God by rejecting his gracious work of conviction in our lives.

On the other hand, some enter the plea, 'guilty'. At a very early age most people learn that negative psychology pays off. To admit guilt often reduces punishment or prevents it altogether. A child will admit to his parent, 'Yes, I did wrong,' and the parent responds by saying, 'That's alright then; just don't do it again.' He avoids the consequences. The sinful heart schemes and thinks that perhaps that will work with God. There are times too when we readily admit our sin and hasten to add: 'Everybody else is doing it.' Somehow, we tend to think that majority opinion will win out in the long run. In this way it is possible to admit sin and guilt without ever coming to repentance. We live in a time when professing Christians readily admit that we are all sinful. They do so, however, with such a matter-of-fact approach that it is evident that the conscience has never been aroused. It is possible to admit sin and yet never be converted.

When the Spirit of God has convicted the conscience, there is fear. Adam, for example, realizing that he had broken the command of God, cried out, 'I heard thy voice . . . and I was afraid' (*Gen. 3:10 KJV*). When the conscience has been aroused, there is fear of God's judgment and wrath. It is that fear that causes a convicted soul to cry out, 'What must I do to be saved?' (*Acts 16:30*). Until that fear drives us to repentance, there is no conversion. When God in his goodness leads us to repentance, some radical changes take place. Formerly, one excused sin and perhaps even laughed about it, now sin becomes too heavy to bear. In Bunyan's *Pilgrim's Progress*, Pilgrim was awakened to his spiritual peril through the ministry of Evangelist, but he continued to bear the burden of sin until he came to the Cross. Evangelist did not quote a 'spiritual law' to remove that burden; Pilgrim bore that burden until the Spirit had wrought his gracious work of conviction and brought him to repentance at the foot of the Cross. It is the goodness of God that leads a man to repentance (*Rom. 2:4*).

In the previous chapter, we drew attention to that difficult passage in Hebrews 6:4–6, 'those who have once been enlightened and have tasted of the heavenly gift and have been made partakers of the Holy Spirit, and have tasted the good word of God and the powers of the age to come, and *then* have fallen away, it is impossible to renew them again to repentance.' There we discussed briefly the enlightening work of the Spirit; now, we must draw attention to the fact that the convicting work of the Spirit is in view also. 'It is impossible to renew them again to repentance.' It is possible for a person to be enlightened in the things of God and convicted by his conscience, and yet not be saved. It is possible to get a few facts in the mind and a few pangs of conscience in the heart and yet not be born into God's family. Though the Spirit of God teach a man and strive with his conscience, that man can still turn away. And, in doing so, he grieves the Spirit of God. Let me emphasize the importance of responding to the convicting work of the Spirit of God; if you do not respond in repentance, your soul will be hardened. One cannot silence the convicting work of God's Holy Spirit without tragic results. Instead of stifling the work of the Spirit in the conscience, learn to deal with sin. Confess it, repent of it, and put it away. As James Buchanan says:

beware of any disposition that may spring up within you, either to quarrel with it as too severe, or to imagine that God cannot or will not enforce it. God's sentence must be a just one, and cannot be reversed, however it may be questioned, by man.[1]

In discussing effectual calling, the Catechism says it is the work of God's Spirit, whereby, *convincing us of our sin and misery*, enlightening our minds in the knowledge of Christ . . . he persuades and enables us to embrace Jesus Christ freely offered to us in the gospel'[2] (my emphasis). The work of the Spirit of God is to convince us of our sin and misery; he does so to bring us to repentance. He enlightens our minds and convicts our conscience through the word of God.

All of this is what the Spirit of God does to bring us to salvation. Again, I ask, what does he do *after* salvation? Does he simply convince us that we are sinners and then leave us on our own?

I shall never forget a night at the beginning of 1944 when I saw myself as a sinner, condemned, and unclean; by faith I looked to Jesus Christ as my Savior. Though I understood only a minimum of truth, there were tears of repentance. But that was not the end of repentance for me. Not too long ago I was reading the scripture, and the Spirit of God reminded me of something in my life I had not dealt with. I had to sit down and write a letter confessing my sin to a couple whom I had offended years ago. I had rationalized it, excused it, and tried to forget it, but the Spirit of God dealt with me until it was set straight. I expect he will bring other things to my attention as I journey along through life. What the Spirit of God does to bring us to salvation, he continues to do after we have come to salvation. He does this in order that we might be sanctified and conformed to the image of Jesus Christ.

The day I was converted I did not know everything about my sinfulness. I still do not! I could, for example, read the commandment, 'Thou shalt not kill,' and think, that is one command I have not broken. As I read the scripture, however, I discover that the root of murder is hatred; that is something I know about! When I understand what the command is saying, I am convicted that I have broken it in my attitude and intention. Further, I discover

[1]*Ibid.*, p. 80.
[2]The Shorter Catechism, Question 31.

that the command not only forbids murder and hatred, it requires something. I discover in Ezekiel that if I do not warn the wicked of his way, his blood will be required at my hand (*Ezek. 3:18*). I might not sin in taking someone's life, but I am guilty of breaking the commandment if I fail to warn the wicked and let him destroy himself. The knowledge of this duty must bring conviction of conscience, and I must repent. The further a man goes on in the Christian life, the more he learns of God's ways. And the more he learns of the law of God, the more sensitive and conscious he becomes of sin. The Spirit of God continues his gracious work of convicting the conscience. I do not mean that the Spirit of God continues to drag skeletons out of the closet; he convicts the conscience of those things which need to be changed and forsaken.

The only way a genuine Christian can have a clear conscience is to confess and forsake sin; we must take our burdens to Calvary. We must take our burden of sin and confess it before our great high priest; our repentance is genuine only if there is a commitment to forsake our sin. 'He who conceals his transgressions will not prosper, but he who confesses and forsakes them will find compassion' (*Prov. 28:13*). The apostle John makes it clear that anyone born of God does not habitually commit sin. When we do sin, 'we have an Advocate with the Father, Jesus Christ the righteous' (*1 John 2:1*). And, when 'we confess our sins, He is faithful and righteous to forgive us our sins and to cleanse us from all unrighteousness' (*1 John 1:9*). Then, 'if our heart does not condemn us, we have confidence before God' (*1 John 3:21*).

The Spirit of God enlightens our minds to bring us to faith, and he convicts our conscience to bring us to repentance. However, as I have pointed out already, I believe it is possible to go as far as that yet not be saved. There is still one more vital step without which there is no true conversion. To that we turn our attention in the next study. These are hard sayings which undoubtedly will cause us much heart searching. With so much superficial Christianity round us, we must 'be all the more diligent to make certain about His calling and choosing you' (*2 Pet. 1:10*).

WHAT WE NEED		Work of the Spirit	To bring
Objective	Subjective		
Revelation	Renewed mind	Enlightens the mind	Faith
Reconciliation	Renewed desires	Convicts the conscience	Repentance
Restoration	Renewed will		

12: *The Application of Redemption (3): The Holy Spirit Renews the Will*

On the day of judgment, no man will be able to point an accusing finger at God and charge him with being unfair. No one will dare say to him, 'You enlightened this man's mind but you left me in darkness; you convicted his conscience but you ignored me. You are unfair and unjust!' There is a sense in which God is at work in the life of every man. Romans chapter 1 tells us that God has given sufficient light in creation so that all men are without excuse. Similarly, Romans chapter 2 says that God has given every man a conscience which witnesses to the fact that the law of God is known to our hearts. It is possible for a man to acknowledge God's existence and to respect his law and yet go his own way. He may follow the light God has given him up to a certain point and then reject it. Though God works a sovereign work of grace in the lives of those whom he has chosen, he does not coerce men into loving him. If the enlightenment of the mind and the conviction of the conscience do not produce true faith and genuine repentance, such operations of God's Spirit increase our condemnation. How can we know if our faith and repentance are genuine? How can we make our calling and election sure?

In our last two studies, we have given only part of the answer to the Catechism question: 'What is effectual calling?' Here is the complete answer: 'Effectual calling is the work of God's Spirit, whereby, convincing us of our sin and misery, enlightening our minds in the knowledge of Christ, and *renewing our wills*, he persuades and enables us to embrace Jesus Christ, freely offered to us in the gospel'[1] (my emphasis). For our calling to be effectual, the Spirit must enlighten the mind, convict the conscience, and

[1]The Shorter Catechism, Question 31.

renew the will. He enlightens the mind to bring us to faith; he convicts the conscience to bring us to repentance; and he renews the will to bring us to obedience. Until the will is renewed and there is the response of obedience, redemption has not been effectually applied. Jesus said, 'He who has My commandments, and keeps them, he it is who loves Me' (*John 14:21*); 'If anyone loves Me, he will keep My Word' (*John 14:23*). The evidence of true conversion is a renewed will, an obedient life.

How does the Spirit of God renew the will? Is this something mystical that just happens for no apparent reason, or is it an objective work of the Holy Spirit? At the outset, we need to understand how the will operates. The will is probably the least understood faculty in man. Many people imagine they know all about the will, but may never have given it any serious thought. There are three basic views of man's will:

1. *The Fatalistic View*. Some years ago, there was a popular song which contained the words: 'Whatever will be, will be.' That is fatalism. The religion of Islam is fatalistic; the Muslim can shrug his shoulders at the turn of events and say, 'It is the will of Allah.' Some extreme views of Calvinism within the Christian church are fatalistic. Whatever the form of fatalism, it creates real problems. If we live in a mechanical universe in which circumstances and events determine our direction and destiny, we are caught in a machine in which we are irresistibly driven to our fate. The bottom line of fatalism is that we really do not have a will at all. Such a position does not match man's experience, however. There are many times when we are aware of the fact that we might have chosen a different course had we desired to do so. Further, if everything is beyond our control, there is no way in which we can be held responsible for decisions and actions. A fatalistic view is inadequate.

2. *The Mystical View*. This is the view that the will of man is completely free, and we are capable, therefore, of complete self-determination. We consider ourselves to be free to do anything we desire. I call this the mystical view because it fails to take some important factors into consideration. If the will of man operates independently and autonomously of any control except our own selfhood, we are pitiable slaves to an irrational and amoral power

operating within us. One can only imagine what would happen if suddenly four billion wills existing on this planet should suddenly decide to operate freely without restraint! It would certainly be chaotic and a foretaste of hell itself; it would be impossible to predict what would happen. Though I believe this is the most widely held and most popular view, it is worse than fatalism. Most people adopt this view because they have never thought about it. It appeals to the unregenerate sinful nature because of the fall; having declared ourselves free of God and autonomous, we like to think we can do exactly as we please. In contrast to fatalism, the mystical view depends on chance. The Bible provides a far better alternative.

3. *The Objective View.* The Bible teaches that God is in sovereign control over all men and yet he has made man a free responsible agent. Whether in a state of innocence prior to the fall, a state of sin, a state of grace, or a state of glory, man is free and responsible. Obviously, it is impossible for us to reconcile God's sovereignty and man's responsibility, but both are clearly taught in the scriptures.

What are the objective factors in the operation of the will ignored by the mystical view? The will does not operate autonomously and independently of the mind and the desires. A man simply cannot choose against, or in opposition to, what he knows and desires. In an earlier chapter I gave two reasons why I am not going to the football match today. First, I do not know if there is a football match to go to. Second, if there were one, I have no desire to go. We might diagram it as follows:

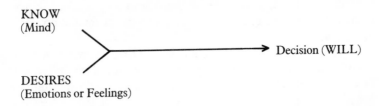

Before the fall, Adam had knowledge of God and love towards God; consequently his mind and his desires were holy and righteous. His decisions, being based on what he knew and desired, were therefore wise and loving.

At the fall, Adam chose not to retain God in his knowledge. Consequently, his knowledge and his desires became self-centered. His decisions were no longer based on wisdom and love but on self-centered knowledge and selfish desires. As a result, his decisions were unwise and unloving. As the apostle Paul says, an unregenerate man lives in the lust of the flesh, doing the desires of the flesh and of the mind (*Eph. 2:3*).

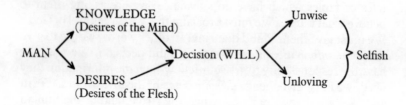

Our Lord taught that a corrupt tree brings forth corrupt fruit; no matter what it does, it cannot, in and of itself, produce good fruit. In other words, it is impossible to get a righteous decision from an unrighteous character. How is it possible then, for a sinner to make a right decision for Christ when that decision is opposed to his own unrighteous character? It is a decision which is completely contrary to his knowledge and his desires. Just as it took a supernatural agent to get Adam to decide against God, it takes another supernatural agent to get sinful man to decide for God. If there is to be a genuine conversion, the Spirit of God must renew the will and thereby enable a person to embrace Jesus Christ.

Failure to understand this has generated all kinds of unbiblical methods in modern evangelism. Manipulative means are employed to 'get decisions'; it is not uncommon to hear popular evangelists declare, 'You can come to Christ by an act of your free will.' Sad to say, the pressure exerted to get people into the kingdom of God is an attempt to get them to make a decision contrary to their knowledge and desires. And they are 'born of the will of the flesh and not of God' (*John 1:13*). Because the function of the will is not understood, many make a false and misleading distinction between accepting Jesus as Savior and accepting him as Lord. Where there is genuine conversion, Jesus is Lord. He is Lord, because where there has been genuine conversion, the will has been renewed unto obedience. But we ask, how does the Spirit renew the will? What means does he use?

First, the will cannot be renewed without the mind being renewed. We cannot call upon men to make a decision for Christ without first presenting the gospel to them; we cannot get men to act upon some truth which the mind has not grasped. Men need to know that the gospel is incontrovertible; it is built upon good and sufficient evidences. We are not asking them to believe old wives' tales or fables which have no substance; we are asking them to believe what is true. We must proclaim the 'whole counsel of God'. We must give them sound doctrine! In other words, we are to give them the *information* they need for a valid decision. We not only have the responsibility to give our fellow-men the information they need, we must give them a *demonstration* of the love of God. Truth and love are the weapons by which the stronghold of the human mind and the human heart are captured. Obviously, this is what *we* are to do; where does the Spirit of God come into the picture?

As we convey the information of God's word, the Holy Spirit brings *illumination*. The Spirit of God enables the sinner to grasp it as the truth. As the Spirit illumines his mind, he sees the evidence as undeniable. When he has information and illumination, he has the right knowledge for a sound or wise decision. He might not be inclined to act upon it, however. His desires must be renewed also. When we give him a demonstration of the love of God, the Holy Spirit brings the *inclination*. As Solomon prayed, 'that He may *incline* our hearts to Himself, to walk in all His ways and to keep His commandments and His statutes and His ordinances' (*1 Kings 8:58*; my emphasis). When information, illumination, demonstration, and inclination come together, the result is *motivation*. With these ingredients, there is the basis for a sound, meaningful decision. When these things come together, the Spirit of God enables a sinner to 'embrace Jesus Christ who is freely offered to us in the gospel'.

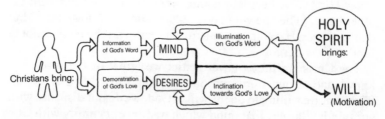

Incidentally, this is one of the wonderful things about preaching the gospel to sinful men. When we come into contact with men, we know it is not by chance; we know that God has caused our paths to cross. We know that, as we are faithful, the Spirit of God is also at work. Such knowledge makes Christian evangelism exciting!

Previously, we emphasized that what the Spirit of God does to bring a person to salvation, he continues to do after salvation. The renewal of the will, just as the enlightenment of the mind and the conviction of the conscience, is not a once-for-all matter. Our Lord spoke to his disciples at Caesarea Philippi and asked them what men said about his identity. They responded by telling him that some thought he was John the Baptist, Elijah, Jeremiah, or one of the prophets (*Matt. 16:14*). Then the Lord turned the question to them, 'Who do you say that I am?' Peter correctly identified him as 'the Christ, the Son of the living God' (*Matt. 16:16*). Such understanding comes from God. 'From that time Jesus Christ began to show His disciples that He must go to Jerusalem, and suffer many things from the elders and chief priests and scribes, and be killed' (*Matt. 16:21*). That was a truth that Peter did not like; he responded by saying, 'God forbid it, Lord!' (Peter's exclamation is a contradiction, incidentally; one cannot say 'God forbid it' and 'Lord' at the same time.)

I confess that many times I have been unwilling to accept what the Lord has said to me, and to do what he has commanded. In fact, I find that my will needs continual renewal. The one thing my sinful nature rebels against is submission to the authority of the

Lord. But the evidence of a regenerate heart is obedience to the Lord's revealed will. 'If anyone loves Me,' says Jesus,'he will keep My word' (*John 14:23*). 'By this we know that we have come to know Him, if we keep His commandments' (*1 John 2:3*). On the other hand, 'The one who says, "I have come to know Him," but does not keep His commandments, is a liar, and the truth is not in him' (*1 John 2:4*).

The Christian life is never static; we 'grow in the grace and knowledge of our Lord and Savior Jesus Christ' (*2 Pet. 3:18*). When we are willing to do the will of God, we do not dispense with our minds. Rather, that mind which was once at enmity with God now comes willingly to be taught by the Spirit of God from the word of God. The desires which were centered in the flesh and antagonistic to God are now set upon the things which are above. The new desire of the heart is to please Christ and exalt his glorious name. There is a basic desire to do what God wants, to be obedient to his will. Naturally, at conversion, we do not know all the will of God. To continue to understand his will, we must grow in knowledge. To continue to desire the will of God, we must grow in grace.

The will of God is revealed in the Bible. Many professing Christians, instead of searching the scriptures to determine what the Lord God requires, make a neat check list of 'do's' and 'don't's'. Often they depend on the pastor or their church to tell them what is right and wrong. Of course, when they come across something they do not like, they begin to look for someone else who has a more convenient check list. Check lists, however, are made by Pharisees for Pharisees. It is possible for a Pharisee to go down his check list, as Saul of Tarsus did, and say, 'As to the righteousness which is in the Law, [I am] found blameless' (*Phil. 3:6*). Saul's life pattern was to keep all the law outwardly, but his heart was not in it. He did many of the right things for the wrong reasons; he did right things but with the wrong motivation. The Bible is not a check list; it is a book of principles, principles which apply to every person in every situation. That means, of course, that as individuals, it becomes our personal responsibility to apply the principles in our own particular circumstances and situations.

Many decisions in life are very complex and difficult to make; we would sooner avoid them or let someone else take the responsibility for them. As responsible beings, however, we must make them. It is always easier to follow the course of least resistance, but, if our will has been renewed by the Spirit of God, we will wrestle in applying the principles of God's word. When we have struggled to determine the principle involved and how it is to be applied, the motive is exposed. For our decisions to be righteous and holy, we must study to show ourselves approved of God, workmen that need not to be ashamed (*2 Tim. 2:15*).

When we discover from the scriptures what God wants us to be and to do, and we do it, then we have found the purpose for which God made us. This is the path to a meaningful life and significant existence.

WHAT WE NEED		Work of the Spirit	To bring
Objective	Subjective		
Revelation	Renewed mind	Enlightens the mind	Faith
Reconciliation	Renewed desires	Convicts the conscience	Repentance
Restoration	Renewed will	Renews the will	Obedience

13: *The Benefits of Redemption*

After the Lord had instructed the rich, young ruler to sell all his possessions, to distribute the proceeds to the poor, and to follow him, he told his disciples that 'it is easier for a camel to go through the eye of a needle than for a rich man to enter the kingdom of God' (*Mark 10:25*). The incident generated a comment from Peter: 'we have left everything and followed You' (*Mark 10:28*). The implication is that since the disciples had left all and followed Jesus, what were they going to get out of it? Perhaps we might have the same question. Having been effectually called by God's Holy Spirit, what is in it for us? Or, as the Catechism asks, 'What benefits do they that are effectually called partake of in this life?' The answer contains three important theological words from which we might be tempted to retreat. Do not let the words frighten you; they tell us something wonderful which should cause the heart of every true believer to rejoice. 'They that are effectually called do in this life partake of justification, adoption, and sanctification, and the several benefits which in this life do either accompany or flow from them.'[1]

The first benefit is *justification*. It was Martin Luther's re-discovery of the doctrine of justification by faith that sparked off the Protestant Reformation. The understanding of this great truth transformed lives, homes, and nations. The dynamic of this doctrine gripped the minds and hearts of multitudes of people at the Reformation to such an extent that the entire course of history was changed. It appears as though most professing Christians today have lost sight of this great doctrine. Our children are taught the nice little formula that 'Jesus died for our sins' without any real

---

[1]The Shorter Catechism, Question 32.

content. In modern evangelism, a 'spiritual law' is often used which says, 'Through him [Jesus] you can know and experience God's love and plan for your life.' This so-called 'law' is totally inadequate. Thomas Watson, one of the Puritan writers, says, 'An error about justification is dangerous, like a defect in a foundation.'[1] It is imperative that we understand what justification is.

'What is justification?' 'Justification is an act of God's free grace, wherein he pardons all our sins, and accepts us as righteous in his sight, only for the righteousness of Christ imputed to us, and received by faith alone.'[2] In Deuteronomy 25:1–2 we read, 'If there is a dispute between men and they go to court, and the judges decide their case, and they justify the righteous and condemn the wicked, then it shall be . . .'. Here is a situation where two men have a disagreement and the matter ends up in court; the case is heard and the judge announces his verdict. The guilty man is condemned and the righteous man is justified. In other words, when the judge makes his pronouncement, it is an act of justice. Having been declared innocent, the righteous man leaves the court-room a free man.

As sinners, there is no question about our guilt before God. We have broken his holy law times without number. In God's court-room there is no evasion of the truth and no perversion of justice. There is no excuse we can give; there is no sin we can hide. We await the verdict though we know what it will be, and we know also that the sentence is death. Just when we see how hopeless our situation really is, the great heavenly Lawyer offers to plead our case. He steps forward to the bar of justice and, acknowledging our guilt, presents his wounded hands and his pierced side as evidence that the penalty or sentence has already been paid in full. On that basis, God the righteous Judge, absolves us of guilt and pronounces us as righteous. We walk from the court-room free men. Of course, if we fail to engage the services of that heavenly Lawyer, all we will be able to do at the final judgment is plead guilty and face the sentence of death.

Suppose we were brought before a court. We have committed some crime and are truly guilty; the whole court knows it. Suppose also that, by some strange turn of events, our lawyer takes out his

[1] Thomas Watson, *A Body of Divinity*, p. 157.
[2] The Shorter Catechism, Question 33.

check book and writes out a check to cover our fine. He pays for the crime we have committed. That is wonderful; we are able to leave the court justified and free.

'Justification is an *act* of God's free grace' (my emphasis). On the basis of the complete work of Jesus Christ, God pronounces us 'not guilty'. We are then justified. Notice what is involved: 'he pardons all our sins'; 'He accepts us as righteous in his sight.' These acts of God on our behalf are not because of any righteousness we might possess (or think we possess!), but 'for the righteousness of Christ imputed to us'. ('Impute' means to charge to one's account.) 'Having been justified,' 'there is therefore now no condemnation for those who are in Christ Jesus' (*Rom. 5:1; 8:1*). Our sins have been pardoned, and we are accepted as righteous. This simple but profound act of justification is the 'good news', the wonderful news of the gospel. God's grace does not end there, however; it is just the beginning.

The second benefit to those who are effectually called is *adoption*. 'What is adoption?' 'Adoption is an act of God's free grace, whereby we are received into the number, and have a right to all the privileges, of the sons of God.'[1] In justification, God clears us of our guilt; in adoption, he takes us into his family. He *receives* us and gives us all the *privileges* of sons. Think of what that means!

Not only are we taken out of the prison, but we are set down at the king's table. Not only are we taken from the swine trough, we get the best calf killed, the shoes for the feet, the ring for the hand, and the best robe of sonship.[2]

There are many who claim to be members of God's family; the Bible makes it clear, however, that only those who have been justified are adopted into his family and may rightly be called his sons. He receives only those who are justified. What privileges do his sons enjoy? As a Father, God loves his children. 'Just as a father has compassion on his children, so the Lord has compassion on those who fear Him' (*Ps. 103:13*). The apostle Paul describes God as 'the Father of mercies and God of all comfort' (*2 Cor. 1:3*). This is illustrated by our Lord in his story of the prodigal son, who

---

[1]*Ibid.*, Question 34.
[2]William P. MacKay, *Notes on the Shorter Catechism* (Edinburgh, Hodder & Stoughton, 1889), p. 96.

having returned to his father was embraced, taken in, and reinstated as a son. An unbiblical emphasis on God's love for all men has, in our day, obscured the truth of God's love for his children. There is a sense in which God loves all men; he is benevolent towards all his creatures. However, we must not forget that 'the wrath of God comes upon the sons of disobedience' (*Eph. 5:6*). We must not forget God's special love for his adopted sons. 'See how great a love the Father has bestowed upon us,' says John, 'that we should be called children of God; and such we are' (*1 John 3:1*). When God redeems us, he sets his love upon us; we become the objects of his particular love.

As a father, God provides for his children. Jesus said, 'If you then, being evil, know how to give good gifts to your children, how much more shall your Father who is in heaven give what is good to those who ask Him!' (*Matt. 7:11*). The Psalmist said, 'The young lions do lack and suffer hunger; but they who seek the Lord shall not be in want of any good thing' (*Ps. 34:10*). God has taken us into his family; as our Father, he provides for all our needs. He does not always give us what we want, of course; he gives us what is best for us. He has our interests at heart.

As a father, God protects his children; 'The angel of the Lord encamps around those who fear Him' (*Ps. 34:7*). Even in the presence of our enemies, he spreads a table before us (*Ps. 23:5*). He is, according to the Psalmist, our refuge and strength, our high tower to which we can flee for security, our shield, and our fortress. 'The eternal God is a dwelling place, and underneath are the everlasting arms' (*Deut. 33:27*). Part of his protection is his guidance. 'He guides me in the paths of righteousness' (*Ps. 23:3*). He guides us with his eye (*Ps. 32:8*), and instructs us in the way we should go (*Ps. 25:9*). 'He will not allow your foot to slip; he who keeps you will not slumber' (*Ps. 121:3*). On occasions, he must discipline us. 'God deals with you as with sons; for what son is there whom his father does not discipline?' (*Heb. 12:7*). Discipline is necessary; it is for our good.

As a father, God keeps his children; 'I give eternal life to them,' said Jesus, 'and they shall never perish, and no one shall snatch them out of My hand' (*John 10:28*). Not one of those who have been justified and adopted into his family is lost.

These are just a few of the basic privileges of being adopted into

God's family. I should point out that both justification and adoption are *acts* of God's grace. Either we have been justified and adopted into the family of God or we are not members of his family. Justification and adoption are not a process. 'As many as received Him, to them He gave the right to become children of God, even to those who believe in His name: who were born not of blood, nor of the will of the flesh, nor of the will of man, but of God' (*John 1:12–13*). We do not become members of God's family by human relationships or tradition; we do not become his sons by human effort or determination. We become his sons when we believe in Jesus Christ and are justified through his death and resurrection and adopted into his family.

Someone has said, 'Never make a goal out of God's starting point.' Being justified and adopted is just the starting point. Having been brought into God's family, we have growth and development ahead of us. That brings us to the matter of *sanctification*. 'What is sanctification?' 'Sanctification is the work of God's free grace, whereby we are renewed in the whole man after the image of God, and are enabled more and more to die unto sin, and live unto righteousness.'[1] In contrast to justification and adoption, sanctification is a *work*. In discussing effectual calling, we saw that what the Holy Spirit does to bring a person to salvation, he continues to do after salvation. He enlightens our minds in the knowledge of Christ, and he continues to do so that we might grow in knowledge. He convicts our conscience, and he continues to do so that we might grow in grace. He renews our will, and he continues to do so that we might become more and more obedient. Why is the Holy Spirit doing this work within us?

We began our study by considering man as God made him. We saw that we are made in God's image as rational beings, moral beings, and beings with purpose. We considered man as sin has made him. We saw that sin has affected the mind, the desires, and the will; it has affected the *whole* man. In considering the offices of Christ, we saw that, as our prophet, priest, and king, he is fully qualified to meet our need exactly. In bringing revelation, he meets our rational need; in bringing reconciliation, he meets our moral need; and in bringing restoration, he gives us purpose. In

---

[1]The Shorter Catechism, Question 35.

effectually calling us, the Holy Spirit renews our minds, our desires, and our wills. In other words, the redemption planned by God the Father, purchased by God the Son, and applied by God the Holy Spirit, is designed to *renew the whole man*. At the outset, God said, 'Let us make man in our image' (*Gen. 1:26*). In effect, Satan said, 'Let us remake man in my image.' In the wonderful plan of redemption, God is 'renewing *the whole man after the image of God*' (my emphasis). God's purpose of redemption, then, is to make us like himself. In writing to the Romans, the apostle Paul said, 'Whom He foreknew, He also predestined to become conformed to the image of His Son' (*Rom. 8:29*). God is remaking his people like himself.

To sanctify means, literally, 'to set apart'. On the one hand, believers are to be set apart *from* their former way of life and from those things which displease God. On the other hand, we are to be set apart *for* God; we are to do his holy will and to glorify and enjoy him. Christian people are unique; their lives are to be characterized by holiness and purity. Sad to say, there are many who 'profess to know God, but by their deeds they deny him, being detestable and disobedient, and worthless for any good deed' (*Tit. 1:16*).

Many years ago, I had the privilege of hearing Dr. A. W. Tozer preach. In his dramatic and inimitable way he said, 'You can take a group of professing Christians today, line them up at the bar of the local tavern, and you wouldn't know they didn't belong there.' God has not called us to be like the world; he has called us to be like him. A story is told of a missionary working in a remote area who had been faithful in telling his native helper about the Lord Jesus Christ. A godly man went to visit the missionary. When he arrived, the native helper answered the door. Seeing the gracious visitor, the helper excused himself to call the missionary. He went to the room where the missionary was working and said in hushed and sincere tones, 'I think the Lord Jesus is at the door.' That is the meaning of sanctification!

Malachi wrote, 'A son honors his father, and a servant his master. Then if I am a father, where is My honor? And if I am a master, where is my respect? says the Lord of hosts' (*Mal. 1:6*). If we truly have been justified and adopted into God's family, we must conduct ourselves accordingly. We are to imitate God as beloved children (*Eph. 5:1*). He is our example; 'you are to be perfect, as your heavenly Father is perfect' (*Matt. 5:48*). That is the goal. If there has been justification and adoption, the evidence will be in God-likeness; there will be growth and development towards the likeness of our Father. Let no one presume that all is well with his soul if there is no evidence of holiness or growth in godliness.

The Catechism question with which we began this study said, 'They that are effectually called do in this life partake of justification, adoption, and sanctification, and the several benefits which in this life do either accompany or flow from them.' 'What are the benefits which in this life do accompany or flow from justification, adoption, and sanctification?' 'The benefits . . . are, assurance of God's love, peace of conscience, joy in the Holy Ghost, increase of grace, and perseverance therein to the end.'[1] Let me comment on each of these briefly:

1. Assurance of God's love. Tragically, in our day, many Christian workers have tried to give people assurance of God's love apart from justification, adoption, and sanctification. Assurance is a benefit which accompanies and flows from these things. Assurance based on any other foundation is without substance; it is presumption. Of course, assurance is not some good feeling; it is the knowledge that we are right with God. That knowledge comes through the word of God. We have assurance of God's love based on what God has said.

2. Peace of conscience. Many people would give all they possess to obtain peace of conscience. One need only look at Martin Luther for a prime example; before he understood justification by faith, he tortured his body unmercifully in a desperate attempt to find peace. Eventually he discovered it is only when we are 'justified by faith, we have peace with God' (*Rom. 5:1*).

3. Joy in the Holy Ghost. Jesus told his disciples, 'These things I have spoken to you, that My joy may be in you, and that your joy may be made full' (*John 15:11*). The Holy Spirit brings the joy of Jesus Christ to the believer. With the assurance of God's love and

[1] The Shorter Catechism, Question 36.

peace of conscience, how can a child of God be without joy? The believer has every reason to 'rejoice in the Lord always' (*Phil.* 4:4).

4. Increase of grace. As we grow in our Christian lives, we become more and more aware of the need for God's grace. How wonderful, in the midst of trials and afflictions, to know that 'My grace is sufficient for you' (*2 Cor.* 12:9). As the song says, 'He giveth more grace when the burdens grow greater.'

5. Perseverance to the end. Jesus said, 'they shall never perish, and no one shall snatch them out of My hand' (*John* 10:28). We are told also in scripture that 'He who began a good work in you will perfect it [or carry it out to completion] until the day of Christ Jesus' (*Phil.* 1:6). Left to ourselves we could never make it; we would slip and fall if our security depended on us. One of the benefits of justification, adoption, and sanctification is that the guarantee which accompanies them is perseverance. Our God will keep his children to the end.

It is my observation that many professing Christians in these days do not enjoy these benefits. It is possible to be a true believer and not possess the assurance of God's love, for example. The lack of assurance in many cases, stems from either ignorance of what God has said or disobedience in doing what God requires. In either case the answer is found in the word of God. Neglect the word of God and assurance will vanish. Similarly, the other benefits are dependent upon the proper consistent use of God's word. Peace of conscience depends upon the knowledge that 'the blood of Jesus His Son cleanses us from all sin' (*1 John* 1:7). Joy in the Holy Ghost is experienced when we know what God has done for us. Increase of grace comes through meditation in God's word. And our perseverance to the end is dependent upon his promise. Therefore, it is imperative to study God's word carefully, to study it systematically, to study it prayerfully, and to study it diligently. Through it, the benefits which accompany or flow from justification, adoption, and sanctification will be yours. God's purpose in giving us these benefits is that we might be like him in mind, desire, and will. This is God's work in the *whole* man to make him *whole*.

PART IV

Remade Men at Work

14: *God's Pattern for the Home*

When we discussed man as God made him, we said that God does not work arbitrarily or experimentally. In creation, God made man for a purpose. The same is true regarding redemption. There is nothing arbitrary or experimental about our salvation; God has a glorious plan in view. It is important to understand that Jesus Christ did not come merely to make salvation *possible*; he came to make it *actual*. If Jesus had come simply to make salvation possible, we could take it or leave it; our salvation would then be dependent upon our whims and the purpose of God would be nullified. That Jesus Christ came to this earth to accomplish a definite and glorious purpose is evident throughout all scripture. One cannot read the Epistle to the Ephesians, for example, without being confronted with the fact that redemption is 'in accordance with the eternal purpose which He [God] carried out in Christ Jesus our Lord' (*Eph. 3:11*). God has not redeemed his people at such tremendous cost simply to be doing something; he redeemed us for a purpose. That means, of course, that he has not redeemed us merely 'to sit on the premises', as someone has said. God has redeemed us to be an active people, people who are committed to and involved in doing his will.

The will of God is personal, practical, and purposeful; it touches every area of our lives. In this chapter, we will concentrate on how it touches the home. The home is the basic unit of society; it was established at creation before either civil government or the church.

In the home, a child receives his values for life, and learns respect for authority and concern for others. The foundation for life is laid in the home. In order that the home might fulfill its function, God has appointed the husband and father as the head.

That does not mean, of course, that he may do as he pleases. Indeed, as I Corinthians 11:3 says, 'Christ is the head of every man.' The man is under authority, and, if he is to lead his household in a meaningful, responsible, and loving way, he must bow to the authority of Christ.

Ephesians chapter 5 emphasizes that the husband is to love his wife 'as Christ also loved the church and gave Himself up for her' (*v.25*). That means that the relationship between Christ and his church is the model or pattern for the home. If the home is going to function as God intends it to function and fulfill its purpose, it must be patterned after the relationship of Christ to his church. What, then, is that relationship? Well, as we have seen, in redeeming his people, Christ 'executes the offices of a prophet, of a priest, and of a king'. The offices of Christ, I believe, form the pattern for the head of the home. As Christ executes these offices in redeeming his church, the head of the home must execute these same offices. This does not imply that the offices of Christ are superseded in any way; there is a sense, however, in which the husband and father must reflect these offices in his relationship to his wife and family. Let us consider each one specifically.

I. THE HUSBAND AND FATHER AS PROPHET

Moses is the great Old Testament example of a prophet. Through him, God revealed his law. That law was, and is, the revelation of God's will for his people. Exodus 32:15 says that God gave Moses two tablets written on both sides. There has been speculation over the centuries as to which of the commandments were on each tablet. It is quite likely that they were duplicates. We know that important documents were duplicated at that time. One copy of the law was to be laid up in the ark of the covenant. It was placed there for safe keeping; it was placed there also as a reminder to men that it was the standard by which men are judged when they come before the throne of God. But having given his law, God did not merely put it away for safe keeping. He did not place it in the ark so that it would be inaccessible to men. (God did not give us a Bible to be placed in a closet either!) Probably one copy of the law was available to men for ready reference. That law became the basis for instruction for each succeeding generation. In Psalm 78:5–7, we read:

124

He established a testimony in Jacob, and appointed a law in Israel, which He commanded our fathers, that they should teach them to their children; . . . that they should put their confidence in God, and not forget the works of God, but keep His commandments.

Each succeeding generation was to be thoroughly instructed in the law of God. Any child deprived of that basic instruction was not equipped for life; if he did not know the law of God, he could not have proper values and priorities. Without the law of God, a person could not help but have a distorted view of himself, others, the creation, and God.

The classical passage on the instruction of children in the law of God is Deuteronomy chapter 6. There we are told that the law of God shall be on *your* heart (*v.6*). That is basic; the law of God must be applied to a man's own life before he attempts to teach it to others. His children will be quick to detect his insincerity and hypocrisy if he tries to teach something he does not practice. The law of God must be written on the heart of the parent first. Then, 'you shall teach them [God's commandments] diligently to your sons' (*v.7*). This was, and is, a chief responsibility of the head of the home. How is the law of God to be taught? You 'shall talk of them when you sit in your house and when you walk by the way and when you lie down and when you rise up' (*v.7*). This was not a matter of rote memorization, though that has its place; *it was the constant and consistent application of the law of God under all kinds of circumstances and on all occasions*. In every aspect of life, the law of God was to be explained to the child. The following verse states that the law was to be bound to the hand and to the forehead. The Jews took that very literally and they bound the law of God to them by the use of phylacteries. It is doubtful if that was God's intention; rather, he was impressing on his people the fact that their thoughts and actions were to be regulated and governed by the law of God. They were even to write the law of God on their doorposts and gates that all who entered their property might know that that particular home was governed by the law of God. Obviously, that kind of teaching requires diligence and discipline, but that is what the Lord God requires. It is the solemn responsibility of God's people to transmit his revelation to their children.

In practical terms, this means that the head of the home must practice what he preaches. It means that he will not commit his child into the hands of pagans to be educated. It means he will exercise careful control over the things his child reads or watches on television. It means also that he will be diligent in leading family devotions and in taking his child to the house of God for regular worship and instruction. 'Fathers,' says the apostle, 'bring [your children] up in the discipline and instruction of the Lord' (*Eph. 6:4*). In other words, the head of the home is to reflect the office of a prophet in seeing that his family is taught the word of the living God.

One of the early editions of the Westminster Confession of Faith, was prefaced by a letter directed 'To the Christian Reader, especially Heads of Families.' It reads in part:

As we cannot but with grief of soul lament those multitudes of errors, blasphemies, and all kinds of profaneness, which have in this last age, like a mighty deluge, overflown this nation; so, among several other sins which have helped to open the flood-gates of all these impieties, we cannot but esteem the disuse of family instruction one of the greatest. The two great pillars upon which the kingdom of Satan is erected, and by which it is upheld, are ignorance and error.

If there be any compassion to the souls of them who are under your care, if any regard of your being found faithful in the day of Christ, if any respect to future generations, labour to sow those seeds of knowledge, which may grow up in after-times.[1]

The head of the home is to reflect the office of prophet in conveying the word of God to his children. He is responsible to see that his children know what the Lord God has said.

II. THE HUSBAND AND FATHER AS PRIEST

When my children were small I used to comment that I had the five biggest proofs of original sin in my home; I probably thought it

[1] Letter attached to The Confession of Faith (reprinted Free Presbyterian Publications, 1976), pp. 3, 6.

sounded smart. I do not say that kind of thing about my children any more, because I have come to understand something of the seriousness of sin. I now realize that only 'fools mock at sin' (*Prov. 14:9*). Sin may never be treated lightly or as a joke. Every child is conceived in sin, born with a rebellious and disobedient nature. There is, of course, only one way that his nature can be transformed. He must confess his sin, repent of it, and embrace Jesus Christ as his personal Savior. Obviously, he will not do that if just left to himself. Consequently, it must be the primary aim of the head of the home to seek the eternal welfare of his entire family. All too frequently parents these days are satisfied if their children become decent citizens, marry into socially acceptable circles, and settle down to a middle-class materialistic existence. Obviously, that is not good enough. No Christian parent can be satisfied to see his child pursue such a course. Surely no Christian can relax spiritually while his children settle down to a mediocre spiritual existence in which the things of God are given mere mental assent or approval.

The big temptation for parents is, of course, to apply pressure to try to coerce children into the kingdom of God. If the parent understands the nature of sin and salvation, he will recognize that it takes more than parental persuasion or manipulation to get children to respond to the things of God. The only way a life can be transformed is by the effectual working of the Holy Spirit in applying the redemption purchased by Christ. When this is understood, the Christian father will recognize his responsibility to function as a priest. *He will appear before God in regular consistent intercession for his family.*

Job was such a man. He rose up 'early in the morning and [offered] burnt offerings according to the number of them all [his children]; for Job said, "Perhaps my sons have sinned, and cursed God in their hearts." Thus Job did continually' (*Job 1:5*). Job was aware that the human heart is easily enticed to lust and sin. After seasons of festivity, Job realized how important it was to bring his children back to serious matters. The thought that they might be tempted to live for pleasure alone drove Job to his knees in intercession for them. Job's fear of God did not end with himself; he sought to keep his children in the fear of God also.

It is a father's privilege and responsibility to pray for his children. For some reason, many fathers fail to be the priest of their family, and the responsibility falls upon the mother; she alone intercedes for the family. Elkanah, for example, was a devout man but, so far as we know, there is no indication that he fulfilled his responsibility in praying for his family. The scripture describes the faithfulness of his wife Hannah, however. Whatever the reason for the silence of Elkanah, the scripture provides a beautiful example of a godly mother praying for her son. In answer to her prayer, God first answered by giving her the child Samuel. As one reads her prayer, it is evident that she had her eye on the purposes of God. Significantly, her prayer contains the first use of the term 'Messiah' ('anointed') in the Old Testament (*1 Sam. 2:10*). After taking Samuel to the temple and devoting him to the service of God, we are told she made a little robe for him each year (*1 Sam. 2:19*). What a picture she presents as she finishes her day's work and then settles down with needle and thread; periodically she holds the garment up to assess the size and to visualize her son in it. Perhaps with every stitch, she prayed. So often the prayers of a faithful mother have been behind a godly man. What a sad contrast the priest Eli makes! We are told that his sons were wicked men who completely disregarded their spiritual responsibilities and lived entirely for themselves. There is no indication whatsoever that Eli ever prayed for his sons or instructed them. He was neither faithful in serving as a prophet nor as a priest. Yet, like every father, as head of the home, he had a special responsibility to serve as the priest of his family.

III. THE HUSBAND AND FATHER AS KING

The world, through the media of television, loves to construe the father of the family as an incompetent blundering fool or else as a tyrant who cannot be tolerated. This caricature of the father is a subtle but effective means of destroying his God-given role. If the authority in the home can be broken down and destroyed, all authority in society is destroyed also. The laws for a king in Israel were clearly stated in Deuteronomy chapter 17. He was to read and to copy the law of God regularly: 'he shall read it all the days of his life, that he may learn to fear the Lord his God . . . that his heart may not be lifted up above his country-men and that he may not turn aside from the commandment' (*vv.19–20*). The same rules apply to the king of the home, at least in principle. The king in the home does not possess ultimate power and is not at liberty to do as he pleases. He is a man under authority whose rule must be regulated by the commandments of God. He is not to allow his heart to be lifted up above his fellow-men, that is, he is not to rule over them in pride or with a spirit of superiority.

A king has the responsibility to see that all the needs of his subjects are met. He is to see that all are given just and equitable treatment. At times he must administer correction and discipline, but he must do so with justice and mercy. Those of us who are parents know how difficult it is to keep all these matters in proper balance. At times we are far too lenient and at other times too severe. Many times we are unreasonable in our demands and are unwilling to admit when we are wrong or unfair. Our rule must be regulated by the commandments of God. Our dealings with our children must be patterned on the way God deals with us.

In the Holy of holies in the tabernacle, the ark of the covenant was housed. On top of it was the mercy seat. The mercy seat was fashioned of pure gold with two cherubim hovering over it to form a kind of canopy. Now, the cherubim were placed there because they were the angelic beings who executed the justice of God. Hence, the throne of God was characterized by mercy (it was the mercy seat) and by justice. Here, they are perfectly blended. Justice and mercy are relative, of course, if they are not based on the objective character of God. In the ark of the covenant, which supported the mercy seat, were three objects: the table of law, Aaron's rod, and a golden pot of manna. The law was derived from God's *truthfulness*; he is 'infinite, eternal, and unchangeable in his . . . truth.'[1] Aaron's rod was placed there because through it God vindicated the leadership of Moses and Aaron. Korah had led a rebellion against them and God caused the rod of Aaron to bud, blossom, and bear ripe almonds; in this way, God confirmed his ordained leadership. Through it, God showed who was right. It was, therefore, a rod of *righteousness*. The golden pot of manna was, of course, a permanent reminder of the way God had provided for the sustenance of his people throughout the wilderness wanderings; it was a constant reminder of God's *faithfulness*.

[1] The Shorter Catechism, Question 4.

My point is that these items in the ark reflect the character of God. Divine justice and mercy are never relative or arbitrary; they are based upon God's truthfulness, his righteousness, and his faithfulness.

Furthermore, the law of God reflects the prophetic office of the Lord, the rod of righteousness reflects his priestly office, and the manna reflects his kingly office. In the home the child is to receive proper instruction in the law of God, righteous representation before the throne of God, and faithful care and discipline in the ways of God. In other words, the character of God as seen in the offices of Christ is to be the basis and pattern for the training of children. How well the head of the home fulfills his role will determine how well prepared the child is to fulfill his role in life. The child who receives proper training in the home will be prepared for his role in the church. And when he functions in the church as he should, other Christians will be prepared for their role in the world.

Because of some modern trends which tend to separate and isolate husband and wife, I should comment about the relationship between the husband/father and the wife/mother. The pattern for their relationship is also derived from the Godhead. 'There are three persons in the Godhead: the Father, the Son, and the Holy Ghost; and these three are one God, the same in substance, equal in power and glory.'[1] Similarly, husband and wife are the same in substance and they are equal in power. But, like the persons of the Godhead, they have different roles. Yet they must be in close agreement. If they disagree it will have a detrimental effect on the children. Parents must be one in their objectives, one in their desires, and one in their activities. It ought to be the most natural thing for a child to look up to his parents and in due time, to look beyond them to their God. According to God's promises we should expect that. In writing to the Romans, Paul asks, 'What advantage has the Jew?' He answers, 'Much every way' (*Rom. 3:1, 2 KJV*). Similarly, we might ask, 'What advantage does a child have when he is born into a Christian home?' 'Much every way!' In the truly Christian home, he receives instruction in the law of God, intercession before the throne of God, and provision and discipline

[1]*Ibid.*, Question 6.

according to the will of God. Surely, there is no better way to prepare him for a meaningful life!

Offices of Christ	Father as head of the home	Objects in the ark	God's justice and mercy based on
Prophet – Revelation	To instruct in the word of God	Law	His truthfulness
Priest – Reconciliation	To intercede before the throne of God	Rod	His righteousness
King – Restoration	To provide for and to discipline in the ways of God	Manna	His faithfulness

15: *God's Pattern for the Church*

Though it is not generally understood or appreciated, there is an important relationship between the home and the church. In Ephesians chapter 5, husbands are instructed to love their wives 'as Christ also loved the church and gave Himself up for her' (*v.25*). And, after discussing the relationship between husbands and wives, the apostle concludes by saying, 'This mystery is great; but I am speaking with reference to Christ and the church' (*v.32*). It is clear that the relationship between husband and wife in the home is to exemplify, illustrate, and demonstrate the relationship which exists between Christ and his church. The pattern and plan that God has for the home, therefore, is essentially the same for the church. In the previous chapter we saw that a child properly trained in the home is prepared for service in the church. If a child has seen the home function as God intended, he will understand how God intends the church to function.

In 1 Corinthians chapter 12 to 14, we are told that God has given gifts to every member of the church; it is clear that those gifts are to be used for the edifying or building up of the church. To describe individual members with their particular gifts, the apostle uses the illustration of eyes and ears. He says, 'if the ear should say, "Because I am not an eye, I am not a part of the body," it is not for this reason any the less a part of the body. If the whole body were an eye, where would the hearing be? If the whole body were hearing, where would the sense of smell be?' (*1 Cor. 12:16–17*). Often the problem is that 'ears' try to function as 'eyes'. That is to say, we try to function in areas for which God has neither equipped nor called us. Gifts are not given to a member to 'do his own thing'; they are not given to create confusion, division, or for the sake of personal advantage. The gifts God has given are to be used for the sake of the church. Sometimes the problem is that some misuse their gifts, others abuse or neglect them, and others simply do not know how to use them. Gifts need to be cultivated and developed. One cannot help but lament the excessive formation of local churches at the present time. There are many towns where one or two churches would be ample and adequate, but instead we find numerous churches, most of which preach the gospel. The sad thing is that so often they compete against each other. The gifts God has given should be used to co-ordinate, unify, edify, and guide the church in the accomplishment of its God-given purpose. Obviously, this does not just happen. As in the home, it depends on the leadership. How well a church functions and fulfills its purpose depends on its leadership.

According to Ephesians chapter 4, one of God's gifts to his church is leadership. Leadership in the church is not to be taken lightly, nor may the qualifications God has laid down for leadership roles be set aside or ignored. The quickest way for the church to depart from its biblical base and God-given purpose is for men to assume responsibility in areas for which they are unprepared and unqualified. Each leader must be called and ordained of God. Incidentally, observe how the leadership of the church is tied to the home. A church leader, we are told, must 'be one who manages his own household well, keeping his children under control with all dignity (but if a man does not know how to manage his own household, how will he take care of the church of God?)' (*1 Tim. 3:4–5*). In other words, if you want to see whether a man is qualified to lead the church, look at his home. As we have seen, Christ executes the offices of prophet, priest, and king; those whom he calls and ordains to lead his church must reflect those same offices.

I. THE TEACHING ELDER OR PREACHER AS PROPHET

While we reject outright the notion that the Pope is the vicar of Christ on earth and possesses the power to make infallible pronouncements, we sometimes find that Protestants tend to go to the other extreme and treat God-ordained leadership with complacency and indifference. Many people seem to consider their preacher as a sort of social 'whipping boy' to be criticized and corrected. Some probably deserve it; especially those who have taken the office to themselves. They claim that God has called them. When God calls, he confirms it in three distinct ways. First, the man himself must be convinced of his call from the word of God. Then, the church of which he is part should endorse his call. That is, the church in which he has been involved knows how sincere he is and what commitment he has; the members there have had opportunity to observe his gifts. They know, better than any others, whether he is suited to the ministry. A good test should be whether his own church would call him as a pastor; if not, they have no business to endorse him for some other church. Finally, his call should be confirmed by a local church which recognizes his gifts and desires him to minister to it. Unfortunately, too many churches have been remiss and have encouraged and endorsed men for the ministry when they should have been bold enough to declare their true conviction that God has not called this or that man to the ministry of God's word.

The call is particularly important because the minister or preacher is to exercise the office of prophet; he is to be the mouthpiece of God. I do not mean that the office of Christ is superseded in any way. He brought a full, complete, and final revelation from God; there is no need for any other. A teaching elder, however, is to reflect that office in declaring the 'whole counsel of God'. According to Ephesians 4:1, teaching elders are God's gift to the church; they are given:

1. 'for the equipping of the saints for the work of service' (v. 12);
2. 'to the building up of the body of Christ' (v. 12);
3. to bring the church to the attainment of unity of the faith in the body (v. 13);
4. to make the church stable so that believers are no longer 'children, tossed here and there by waves, and carried about by every wind of doctrine' (v. 14); and
5. to bring spiritual development and growth so that the church may come to 'the knowledge of the Son of God, to a mature man, to the measure of the stature which belongs to the fulness of Christ' (v. 13).

The teaching elder is to build up his congregation to the point where the members do 'the work of service'. It is his responsibility to stand before his people and declare the word of God without fear, doubt, or compromise. He is to declare 'what man is to believe concerning God, and what duty God requires of man'.[1] He must expound the truth of God's word and explain its principles so that each member will know what to do and how to do it in his particular circumstances.

Not many people these days take the sacred office of teaching elder very seriously. Too often other matters demand time and attention and church members fail to attend to the word of God as it is delivered at appointed times through the servant he has sent them. Many people stay at home from church to be well enough to go to work or to school; the word of God is not important to them.

It is clear in the Old Testament that when God sent a prophet, he expected people to pay attention. Giving attention to the preaching of God's word is no less important in the new dispensation. It is not a matter of personal preference; if God is speaking, we must listen. Of course, there are times when members object to what the preacher says. Some just find him boring. Such problems show us all the more reason a church ought to give careful attention to the preacher it calls. Once a man has been called and the people say, 'This is God's servant; we want him to be our minister,' they have no right to 'lift up their hand against the Lord's anointed'. Of course, through human frailty, mistakes may be made by both minister and congregation. Grace and patience may be required by both. But, when a church has called a minister, members are not at liberty personally to oppose his ministry. If this is not so, the call of God means nothing.

When a person joins a church, he places himself under the instruction of that church; he declares publicly that he is willing to receive the word of God from that pulpit. (For that reason, he ought to know what the church stands for before he joins.) There are times when he is not going to like what he hears. He might even feel like stoning the prophet of God but, if that prophet is faithful and true to the word of God, no member ought to turn away and go to another church. Sometimes the proclamation of the word of God demands reproof and correction; that is never easy to take, but it might be the very thing that is needed at a particular time.

[1] The Shorter Catechism, Question 3.

The word of God may not be dismissed on the basis of personal whim or fancy.

Of course, we do not forget that there may be false prophets. According to Deuteronomy chapter 13, we are not to listen to the words of anyone whose teaching conflicts with the law of God. Numbers chapters 22 to 24 provides the record of that unusual man, Balaam. He is described as a prophet of the Lord and, indeed, he made some important Messianic predictions. However, having been offered rich reward by the king of Moab, he endeavored to curse the people of God. Every time he attempted to do so, he blessed them instead. Failing to curse Israel and having missed the reward, he devised another way to accomplish the same end. From what we can determine, he instructed the women of Moab to entice the men of Israel to sin. At the same time, he reminded Israel that, since they were God's chosen people, they could sin without fear of punishment or retribution.

Balaam's teaching is summarized in Revelation 2:14. There, the Lord says to the church at Pergamum, 'you have there some who hold the teaching of Balaam, who kept teaching Balak to put a stumbling block before the sons of Israel, to eat things sacrificed to idols, and commit acts of immorality.' Because of Balaam's distorted message, Israel fell into grievous sin and, as an immediate result, twenty-four thousand Israelites perished. Soon after, the prophet himself was slain. The case of Balaam illustrates the tragedy of a prophet (or teaching elder) who modifies, twists, adulterates, or perverts the message of God. It is a sad reminder that not all who occupy the sacred office are faithful. It is so easy to accommodate the message for the sake of popularity or personal gain. A true prophet, in contrast, will reflect his Lord. Like Jesus, he does not speak from himself; he comes to declare what he has received from God. And when that word is proclaimed faithfully, God's people must pay careful attention; God will hold them responsible for what they do with his word.

II. THE DEACON AS PRIEST

Since Jesus has 'opened for us a new and living way' into the presence of God, we do not need another priest. Our Lord has made it possible for us to 'draw near with confidence to the throne of grace' (*Heb. 4:16*). He alone is our mediator; he 'always lives to make intercession for' us (*Heb. 7:25*). And yet, though he represents us, he has made us a 'kingdom of priests'. The scripture teaches the priesthood of all believers. As priests we have the right, indeed, the responsibility, to approach God on behalf of others. And, of course, whenever we intercede on behalf of others, we are reflecting the priestly office of Christ. While we all have responsibility here, there are some within the church who are specifically called to this ministry.

A priest is described as one who deals 'gently with the ignorant and misguided' (*Heb. 5:2*). Isaiah described the Lord when he said, 'He shall feed his flock like a shepherd: he shall gather the lambs with his arm, and carry them in his bosom, and shall gently lead those that are with young' (*Isa. 40:11 KJV*). He is a compassionate high priest. Some within the church are given special gifts to care for those in need. In the early church, certain men were chosen as deacons to relieve the apostles of the burden of practical needs within the congregation. They were men filled with the Holy Spirit, called of God to a compassionate and sympathetic ministry of caring. Deacons are to be involved in acts of mercy; they must, therefore, be acquainted with the physical and material needs of the congregation. When they are aware of those needs, they are in a unique situation to pray on behalf of others. Since some of those personal needs cannot be made public, they have a unique responsibility to intercede for others.

In addition to the element of intercession, the deacon reflects the office of priest in another way. He is required to make a grateful sacrifice of himself, for the sake of others. In this, too, he reflects the office of priest. The scripture warns that they must 'first be tested; then let them *serve* as deacons if they are beyond reproach . . . those who have *served* well as deacons obtain for themselves a high standing and great confidence in the faith that is in Christ Jesus' (*1 Tim. 3:10, 13*; my emphasis). In serving well, a deacon is like his Lord, who 'did not come to be served, but to serve' (*Matt. 20:28*).

Cain is presented to us as an unfaithful priest. When he offered his own sacrifice, he tried to do it in his own way. Because he completely disregarded the instructions God had evidently given, his sacrifice was unacceptable to God. His brother, Abel, however, was obedient and faithful. Although Abel had done nothing to offend Cain, Cain was infuriated and murdered Abel. Cain broke both the first commandment to love the Lord God with all his heart, and the second commandment, to love his neighbor as himself (*Luke 10:27*). In disregarding God and destroying his brother, Cain illustrates all that a priest should not be. It is a tragic reminder of the fact that not every deacon is sufficiently concerned to pray for the needy; not every deacon is prepared to sacrifice that the needs of others might be met. The true and faithful deacon will reflect his Lord both in character and in the way he performs his responsible work. Of course, if a deacon is to fulfill his function properly, he must have the support of the church behind him.

III. THE RULING ELDER AS KING

Jesus Christ is king of the church. He has been exalted to the right hand of God and all authority and power have been placed under his feet. No man can usurp that authority, though many have tried! As king of the church, our Lord has decreed that his church be ruled 'properly and in an orderly manner' (*1 Cor. 14:40*). In order that the church operate smoothly and effectively, he has called and ordained men who are to reflect his kingly office. They are, of course, the ruling elders.

If the church is to glorify her Lord and carry out his purpose, two areas must be watched constantly. The first is *unity*. In writing to the Corinthians, Paul said, 'I hear that divisions exist among you' (*1 Cor. 11:18*). That was a problem not to be tolerated. In Paul's letter to the Philippians, he exhorted two ladies, Euodia and Syntche, to 'live in harmony in the Lord' (*Phil. 4:2*). To the Ephesians, he wrote, 'being diligent to preserve the unity of the Spirit in the bond of peace' (*Eph. 4:3*). He warned the church at Rome to 'keep your eye on those who cause dissensions and hindrances contrary to the teaching which you learned' (*Rom. 16:17*).

Division within the body of Christ is a serious matter. In the first temptation of our Lord, it is clear that he did not come to obtain kingdoms (plural) but to purchase *a* kingdom. The kingdom of Christ must not be divided. Of course, we are speaking here about the true universal church; some churches become apostate and, as our Lord himself declared, they become 'synagogues of Satan' (*Rev. 2:9*). When that happens, they cannot be numbered as true churches. That, however, is another matter. Disunity within the body cannot be tolerated. We need to understand that that does not mean organizational unity necessarily; it does mean organic unity. At the supermarket, one might find oranges neatly arranged; that is organizational unity. On the orange tree, the fruit is distributed all over the tree, but that fruit has an organic unity; they have a common life. The ruling elders of a local church are to watch lest the unity of their body be interrupted or destroyed. When there is any indication that the unity is threatened, they are to act decisively according to biblical principles.

The ruling elders are responsible also for the *purity* of the church in both teaching and life. There is, of course, a close relationship between belief and behavior, or faith and practice. Any church which relaxes its teaching of doctrine, will soon relax its practice of living also. The elders must watch for any deviation in doctrine or decline in morals. If any issue arises, they must use discipline in order to correct the problem.

Many people these days have an exclusively negative concept of discipline. It should be remembered that the words 'discipline' and 'disciple' have the same root. Discipline takes several forms and is designed to make disciples. When a person joins a church fellowship, he places himself under the 'nurture and discipline' of that church. When the elders act to correct in doctrine or reprove in behavior, the member must submit as unto the Lord. The Lord's word is clear: 'Obey them that have the rule over you, and submit to them: for they watch in behalf of your souls, as they that shall give account; that they may do this with joy, and not with grief: for this were unprofitable for you' (*Heb. 13:17 ASV*).

It is the responsibility of the ruling elders to examine prospective church members; they must determine the validity of their Christian experience and of their personal commitment to Jesus Christ. To admit anyone on any other basis does neither the church nor the individual any favor. The individual gains a false sense of security and the church gains a potential problem. One member living in sin is a disgrace to the entire congregation, and any action taken by the elders must be done for the good of the whole church.

The Old Testament records the story of a prince in Israel by the name of Korah, who gathered 250 followers around him and challenged the leadership of Moses and Aaron (*Num. 16*). He accused Moses of having made himself the leader. He declared, 'You have gone far enough, for all the congregation are holy, every one of them, and the Lord is in their midst; so why do you exalt yourselves above the assembly of the Lord?' (*Num. 16:3*). Korah refused to recognize that God had called and ordained Moses and Aaron to their respective offices of leadership. He failed to realize that all the congregation were not holy; not all of Israel were spiritually mature and capable of wise decisions. He failed to understand that not everyone knows what his gifts are and how to exercise them properly. And even if all Israel had been spiritually mature, it would have been destructive to let everyone go his own way and 'do his own thing'. The land could never have been occupied and the enemies defeated if everyone had acted individually. Neither in Israel in the Old Testament nor in the church in the New Testament, was democracy the system of government. The church stands under the authority of Jesus Christ; as the king of the church, he calls and ordains men to lead and rule his people. Those who rebel against God-ordained leadership, rebel against God (see *Exod. 16:8*). Leadership in the church is a serious matter; for that reason, we must be careful never 'to lay hands on any man suddenly' or carelessly.

In discussing the leadership in the church, we have used three negative examples: Balaam as a false prophet, Cain as a false priest, and Korah as a false king. God places them together as a trio of ancient apostates in the little Book of Jude. We are told about apostates who had 'gone the way of Cain, and for pay they have rushed headlong into the error of Balaam, and perished in the rebellion of Korah' (*Jude 11*). These three are the opposite of what is required in a prophet, priest, and king. Compare 'the way of Cain' with Jesus who is 'the Way'. Compare 'the error of Balaam' with Jesus, 'the Truth'. And, compare 'the rebellion of Korah' with Jesus, 'the Life'. These three individuals serve to remind us that we need to be alert to falsehood and deception in the church. This trio serves to remind us that the church needs men who reflect the offices of Christ. Also, they serve to remind us that the quickest way to destroy the impact of the church is to place wrong men in office. Never before has it been more important for the church leadership to exemplify the character and offices of the Lord Jesus Christ.

When church leadership reflects the offices of Christ, the church will be effective in 'equipping the saints for the work of the ministry' and in reaching the lost world for Christ. The effectiveness of the church is directly proportionate to the extent to which we practice biblical principles of church leadership. Every church member who is serious about the ministry of the church should be in regular and consistent prayer for the leaders of his church. They must give account to God for the souls of members and for souls in their community.

Offices of Christ	Offices in church	For purpose of	Negative examples
Prophet **– Revelation**	Teaching elder	Instruction	Balaam (*Num. 22–24*)
Priest **–Reconciliation**	Deacon	Caring Intercession	Cain (*Gen. 4*)
King **– Restoration**	Ruling elder	Direction Discipline	Korah (*Num. 16*)

16: *God's Plan for the World*

When I was a child it was popular to collect autographs. In one of my autograph books, one person wrote the word 'Salvation'. Underneath, he wrote:

> The Father thought it
> The Son bought it
> The Spirit brought it
> The Bible taught it
> The devil fought it
> And I got it.

Though novel, that contains a lot of sound theology. It implies that God has a great comprehensive plan. There is, however, one important ingredient missing. It fails to include the role of the church in proclaiming it. Sad to say, that aspect is not only missing from this autograph entry, it is missing from the thinking of many Christian people in these days. We have thought of the great commission of our Lord as a personal and individual responsibility only, and overlooked the fact that the manifold wisdom of God is made known through the church (*Eph. 3:10*). Further, many have overlooked the fact that the 'church is the pillar and support of the truth' (*1 Tim. 3:15*). Basically, that means the church is responsible for the preservation and proclamation of the truth of God's word. God has not called Christians to 'do their own thing'; he has saved individuals to be part of a body in which each one exercises the gifts God has given him for the good of all. Without the unity of the body, there is no cohesion among the members, no sense of responsibility to other members, and no orderly proclamation of the gospel to the lost world. The world without Christ stands under God's wrath and curse; it awaits his judgment. God has, however, given to his church the responsibility to warn the world to 'flee from the wrath to come' (*Matt. 3:7*). So then, let us consider the following God-given responsibilities of the church to the world.

I. THE CHURCH MUST PROCLAIM THE LAW OF GOD
WITH A PROPHETIC VOICE

If the world is to be aroused to its peril, it must be confronted by the demands of the law of God. The world must realize where and how God is offended; people must know they have 'sinned and fall short of the glory of God' (*Rom. 3:23*). This is essential because men must see their spiritual predicament before they can understand their need. Sinners cannot be called to repentance by telling them simply that 'God loves them and has a wonderful plan for their lives'. John Wesley said,

One in a thousand may have been awakened by the gospel: But this is no general rule: The ordinary method of God, is to convict sinners by the Law, and that only.[1]

Indeed, the law is 'our schoolmaster to bring us to Christ' (*Gal. 3:24 KJV*). Of course, sinful men object to God's law; they do not see its value. As John Newton said,

We cannot be at enmity with God, and at the same time approve of his law; rather this is the ground of our dislike to him, that we conceive the law by which we are to be judged as too strict in its precepts, and too severe in its threatenings; and therefore men, so far as in them lies, are for altering this law. They think it would be better if it required no more than we can perform, if it allowed us more liberty, and especially if it was not armed against transgressors with the penalty of everlasting punishment.[2]

Actually, there is no gospel to offer until men see their need. And to awaken men to their need, the church must declare without fear, doubt, or compromise 'what man is to believe concerning

---

[1] John Wesley, *Sermons on Several Occasions*, p. 424.
[2] John Newton, *Letters of John Newton* (London, Banner of Truth Trust, 1960), p. 44.

God and what duty God requires of man.'[1] The church must proclaim the law of God clearly. When the world is awakened to its peril, then we must freely, authoritatively, and genuinely offer Jesus Christ, who is presented to us in the gospel.

The church is to give a clear proclamation of the revelation. The scripture asks, 'How then shall they call upon Him in whom they have not believed? And how shall they believe Him whom they have not heard? And how shall they hear without a preacher? And how shall they preach unless they are sent?' (*Rom. 10:14–15*). Who exactly is responsible? Is it the pastor? Is it the missionary who is sent by the church? Indeed, both the pastor and the missionary are involved, but the task of evangelism is not confined to them. The proclamation of the word of God is the responsibility of the entire church. God has given teaching pastors to the church in order that the saints might be built up to the place where *they* do the work of the ministry (*Eph. 4:11*). When members of a church have been properly instructed, cared for, and disciplined, they are 'equipped for every good work' (*2 Tim. 3:17*). If the church is going to speak the law of God authoritatively to a lost and unbelieving world, it must not be unstable and tossed to and fro by every wind of doctrine (*Eph. 4:14*). The church must be strong if she is to do exploits (*Dan. 11:32*). In his wisdom, God has placed his people in offices, factories, market places, educational institutions, court-rooms, and political positions where they are in constant contact with ungodly people. He has placed them there to challenge and influence the world. The life of the Christian in the world should be a rebuke to unrighteousness; it should be an example in justice, righteousness, and truth. What an impact the church could have if Christians voiced biblical convictions where they work! The conscience of the world needs to be disturbed; today, the world cheats in business and on income tax, engages in the murder of the unborn, perverts sex in the most wicked ways, and exploits the creation without any pangs of conscience, because of the guilty silence of the church. The law of God must be proclaimed and lived, not just by preachers and missionaries but by all who profess the name of Jesus Christ.

God does not call his servants to frustration and futility; he calls us to faithfulness. There are many, however, who are frustrated in

[1]The Shorter Catechism, Question 3.

their employment and in their personal circumstances. There are times, of course, when God brings frustration and dissatisfaction to move us. We need to realize, however, that God never places his servants in situations by chance. Sometimes he places us in difficult situations to bring us into contact with sinners and to give us the opportunity to demonstrate how the law of God works under stress. When we understand this, it does two things for the Christian. The realization of God's placement of us brings a sense of *responsibility*. Though circumstances might be frustrating, if God has placed his servant there, it is vital that the servant be found faithful. Complaining will give way to diligence. Secondly, the realization of God's placement of us brings *confidence*. God's placement of a servant in a difficult situation means that God has a work for him or her to do there. If this truth were understood by Christians, the church would have a tremendous impact on the world.

When the Lord Jesus was taken into the wilderness to be tempted by the devil, Satan challenged him to turn stones into bread to meet his physical need. The Lord responded by saying, 'Man shall not live on bread alone but on every word that proceeds out of the mouth of God' (*Matt. 4:4*). As the great Prophet, Jesus came to declare God to men. He came to reveal what the Lord God requires of his creatures. To fulfill that prophetic office, he had to speak the word of God with conviction, authority, and power. To have yielded to the temptation would have meant that he doubted God's word; it would have meant that he no longer considered God's word reliable and trustworthy. Had he yielded, he would have disqualified himself from the prophetic office. The temptation our Lord faced is the same temptation that faces the church. It is a temptation to become overly concerned about physical and material things and to forget that the church's primary responsibility is to fulfill a prophetic role in declaring the law of God to an unbelieving world. Unfortunately, too often churches have lost sight of priorities and of their commission and have disqualified themselves from their prophetic role.

II. THE CHURCH MUST EXPRESS THE LOVE OF GOD WITH A PRIESTLY HEART

The love of God was expressed in Jesus Christ at Calvary. That same love is to be expressed to the world through disciples in the church. If 'God so loved the world, that He gave His only begotten Son' (*John 3:16*), how can the church do less? Love for the world must be expressed in sacrifice and prayerful concern. How can professing Christians hoard possessions and strive to build material empires when men made in the image of God are lost? How can we profess to love God when we shut up our hearts of compassion to men who are in need? Surely, 'the love of Christ controls' true believers (*2 Cor. 5:14*). The person who really knows God will say with the apostle, 'I am under obligation both to Greeks and to barbarians, both to the wise and to the foolish' (*Rom. 1:14*). Such a priestly concern is not generated by entertaining programs or stewardship appeals; it comes from a heart that is in love with Jesus Christ. Of course, the love of God is not some romantic or sentimental notion; it is an objective concern born out of proper instruction, nurture, and discipline. If the church fulfills its role to its membership properly, it will produce people who take the condition of the world seriously and who will commit themselves to sacrificial living, systematic giving, and prayerful involvement. Unfortunately, too often the responsibility falls on a few individuals whose hearts the Lord has touched. Occasionally, one finds a church that has learned to love sacrificially; one can only imagine what would happen if the church in general took the word of God seriously and acted accordingly. What an impact the church would have if every professing Christian proclaimed the law of God clearly and expressed the love of God fervently!

Love is expressed in sacrifice and prayerful concern. A striking example is that of Hannah. When Hannah prayed that the Lord would give her a 'man-child' she was asking for something more than the removal of her reproach. For about four hundred years Israel had been without leadership and 'every man did what was right in his own eyes' (*Judg. 17:6*). Hannah was broken-hearted over the condition of her nation; she was sickened by the idolatry, immorality, apostasy, anarchy, and violence. I believe she desired a 'man-child' who, under God, would do something about the problems in the nation. As we noticed earlier, her song of thanksgiving, in 1 Samuel chapter 2 shows that she had her heart fixed on the coming of the Messiah.

Hannah's concern grew out of her understanding of the purposes of God. Her concern was expressed in her prayer. The name 'Samuel' means 'heard of God'. Hannah did not merely pray for a son and then leave it at that. As soon as her child was weaned, she gave him to the Lord to serve him all the days of his life (*1 Sam. 1:11*). In other words she was prepared to make the sacrifice; she was prepared to give her son for the fulfillment of God's purpose. With that kind of prayerful concern and sacrifice, it is little wonder that, before long, 'all Israel from Dan even to Beersheba knew that Samuel was confirmed as a prophet of the Lord' (*1 Sam. 3:20*). Nor is it surprising that every time a crisis arose, Samuel was on his knees. Samuel said, 'Far be it from me that I should sin against the Lord by ceasing to pray for you; but I will instruct you in the good and right way' (*1 Sam. 12:23*). His concern and love for the people were expressed in intercessory prayer. God has used such men and women in the past; no doubt he will use others in time to come. But why should they be the exception rather than the rule?

The second temptation of our Lord recorded by Matthew was to cast himself down from the pinnacle of the temple. Satan assured Christ that he had scriptural authority for doing this. It was, of course, a temptation to do something spectacular or sensational to attract the attention of the people. The temple authorities had shown complete indifference to the coming of Jesus. If he were to do something dramatic, they would take notice. But Jesus did not come to bring sensation; he came to bring salvation.

One of Jesus' first official acts in Jerusalem was to cleanse the temple. At that time, the officials asked him for a sign. He responded by saying that the sign he would give was, 'Destroy this temple, and in three days I will raise it up' (*John 2:19*). In commenting, John says, 'He was speaking of the temple of His body' (*v.21*). And, when 'He was raised from the dead, His disciples remembered that He said this' (*v.22*). The reason why Jesus identified himself with the temple was that it served to point to his priestly work. The sacrifices, the priests, the furnishings, and materials all foreshadowed his person and work. When Jesus had offered himself as a sacrifice for sins forever, the temple became obsolete. The temptation was, of course, to avoid the sacrifice. Had Jesus jumped from the pinnacle of the temple, he would have attracted the attention and won the admiration of the people, but he would have disqualified himself as a compassionate high priest, a priest with such love that he gave his own life for the life of his people.

Is not this the same temptation that we face in the church today? We are anxious to impress the crowds with our facilities and programs; we try to do things that will be spectacular and sensational. It is doubtful, however, if the world has ever been impressed with our self-image. The world will be impressed only when it sees the genuine expression of the love of God. God says,

If my people, which are called by my name, shall humble themselves, and pray, and seek my face, and turn from their wicked ways; then will I hear from heaven, and will forgive their sin, and will heal their land (*2 Chron. 7:14 KJV*).

The church must not substitute things of her own devising for her priestly role in the world.

III. THE CHURCH MUST DEMONSTRATE THE POWER
OF GOD WITH KINGLY AUTHORITY

When the army of Israel was paralyzed by fear of a defiant giant, it seemed absurd to think that a mere shepherd boy, without training or armor, should accept the challenge to fight. As David went forth against Goliath, David said, 'You come to me with a sword, a spear, and a javelin, but I come to you in the name of the Lord of hosts, the God of the armies of Israel' (*1 Sam. 17:45*). Today, the church is confronted by many giants; the giant of humanism, for example, comes with all kinds of weapons and resources. Whenever humanism issues its challenge, every man flees from him and is sore afraid (*1 Sam. 17:24*). Worse still, many compromise. A church elder once confronted me and said, 'Surely you don't expect to solve people's problems from the Bible!' He himself was proud of his ability as a counselor. To my knowledge, he had never helped anyone, but he knew all the latest techniques. He had completely forgotten that the gospel 'is the power of God for salvation' (*Rom. 1:16*). Like many, he had ignored or forgotten the power of the name of God.

On the other hand, there are groups in the church today which claim to have the power of God and are able to do signs and miracles. Many are impressed by their demonstrations. No doubt many are sincere, and do not realize that they have usurped authority delegated to apostles alone (see *2 Cor. 12:12*). More than that, their methods and results are not particularly impressive. Our Lord said there will be many who will say, 'Lord, Lord, did we not prophesy in Your name, and in Your name cast out demons, and in Your name perform many miracles?' And then I will declare to them, 'I never knew you; depart from Me, you who practice lawlessness' (*Matt. 7:22–23*). Apparently they are people who have been fooled by demonstrations of power. In John 2:23 we read that 'many believed in His name, beholding His signs which He was doing'. John makes clear in the following verses that their faith was not genuine. In commenting, George Hutcheson says, 'It is a clear evidence of unsoundness when Christ's works are the chief thing drawing men to profess faith, and not his word.'[1] Signs do not build conviction or commitment; they last only so long as no one else comes along and does something more intriguing or captivating.

The greatest demonstration of the power of God is the transformation of a sinner into the image of Jesus Christ. God's power is demonstrated when an alcoholic is liberated from the bondage of sin. The power of God is seen when 'the works of the flesh' are replaced by the 'fruit of the Spirit'. It is seen as 'we are enabled more and more to die unto sin and live unto righteousness.'[2] Often the path of the righteous is filled with conflict and adversity; it was so in the case of Job. One purpose God has in allowing suffering and affliction to come to the righteous is to demonstrate his grace. Suffering and affliction will show whether faith is real and whether the power of God works. In that respect, trial and tribulation are necessary; one cannot talk about the grace and power of God with authority if they have not been proved. Paul says, 'Those who receive the abundance of grace and of the gift of righteousness will *reign in life* through the One, Jesus Christ' (*Rom. 5:17*; my emphasis). The world has an unanswerable testimony of the power of God when it sees a Christian reigning in

---

[1]George Hutcheson, *John* (London, Banner of Truth Trust, 1972), p. 39.
[2]The Shorter Catechism, Question 35.

life in the midst of adversity. The power of God is demonstrated in godly living.

The third temptation of our Lord took place on a high mountain where the devil showed him all the kingdoms of the world and said to him, 'All these things will I give You if you fall down and worship me'. In reply, Jesus said to him, 'Begone, Satan! For it is written, "You shall worship the Lord your God, and serve Him only"' (*Matt. 4:10*). The meaning of worship is, of course, to recognize 'worth-ship'. Satan wanted Jesus to recognize his worth. Being the deceiver, he told only half the story; he said nothing about service. Jesus put things back into perspective; worship always involves service. To have recognized Satan's worth would have resulted in service to Satan. Had our Lord yielded to this temptation, he would have abdicated his kingly office. Instead of exercising and demonstrating his power, he would have demonstrated his weakness.

Is not this the problem in the contemporary church? We think we may worship God without serving him. We say we recognize the worth of our King, but we fail to do what he says. The power of God is most clearly demonstrated when we 'worship in spirit and in truth', and having recognized his worth, we go forth to serve him obediently and faithfully. The power of God is expressed in practical godly living. Paul wrote,

He has said to me, 'My grace is sufficient for you, for power is perfected in weakness.' Most gladly, therefore, I will rather boast about my weaknesses, that *the power of Christ may dwell in me* (*2 Cor. 12:9*; my emphasis).

As we have discussed the role of the church in the world, we cannot help but be grieved over the fact that the church is having very little impact on the world at the present time. The world is scarcely even aware of the church's existence, and when it is aware, few people would stop to consider that it might have answers to the questions and issues of life. Certainly there is need for genuine revival in the church. Not until the church returns to biblical principles and to its biblical purpose, will it become effective again. The Psalmist prayed:

God be merciful unto us, and bless us; And cause his face to shine upon us; That Thy way may be known upon earth, Thy salvation among all nations. . . . God shall bless us; and all the ends of the earth shall fear him (*Ps. 67:1–2, 7 KJV*).

May God give us the wisdom, grace, and strength to fulfill our purpose in society by proclaiming the law of God clearly, by expressing the love of God fervently, and by demonstrating the power of God authoritatively. Obviously, we cannot accomplish this with human resources or human strength. We shall fulfill the purpose for which God made us only as we are being transformed by his grace into his image.

Offices of Christ	The church is to	Temptation
Prophet **– Revelation**	Proclaim the law of God	Command stones to be turned into bread
Priest **– Reconciliation**	Express the love of God	Jump from the pinnacle of the temple
King **– Restoration**	Demonstrate the power of God	Worship for the kingdoms of the world